SUPER EASY SONGBOOK

CLASSICAL

T0066486

ISBN 978-1-4950-7392-2

HAL•LEONARD®

7777 W. BLUEMOUND RD. P.O. BOX 13819 MILWAUKEE, WI 53213

In Australia Contact:
Hal Leonard Australia Pty. Ltd.
4 Lentara Court
Cheltenham, Victoria, 3192 Australia
Email: ausadmin@halleonard.com.au

Visit Hal Leonard Online at
www.halleonard.com

Welcome to the *Super Easy Songbook* series!

This unique collection will help you play your favorite songs quickly and easily. Here's how it works:

- Play the simplified melody with your right hand. Letter names appear inside each note to assist you.

- There are no key signatures to worry about! If a sharp ♯ or flat ♭ is needed, it is shown beside the note each time.

- There are no page turns, so your hands never have to leave the keyboard.

- If two notes are connected by a tie ⌣, hold the first note for the combined number of beats. (The second note does not show a letter name since it is not re-struck.)

- Add basic chords with your left hand using the provided keyboard diagrams. Chord voicings have been carefully chosen to minimize hand movement.

- The left-hand rhythm is up to you, and chord notes can be played together or separately. Be creative!

- If the chords sound muddy, move your left hand an octave* higher. If this gets in the way of playing the melody, move your right hand an octave higher as well.

  * *An octave spans eight notes. If your starting note is C, the next C to the right is an octave higher.*

ALSO AVAILABLE

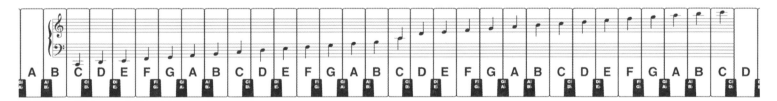

Hal Leonard Student Keyboard Guide HL00296039

Key Stickers HL00100016

Air
from Water Music

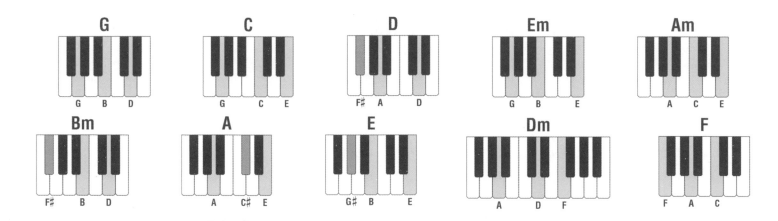

By George Frideric Handel

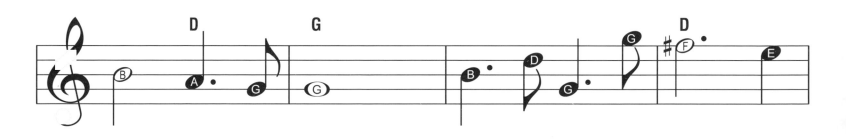

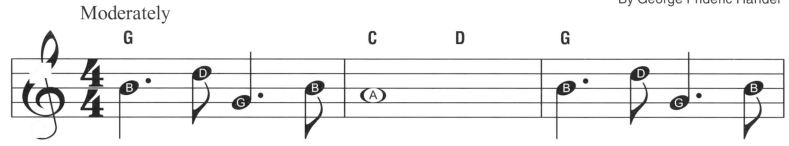

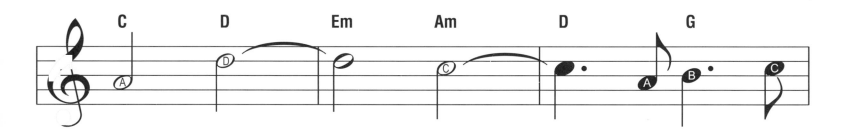

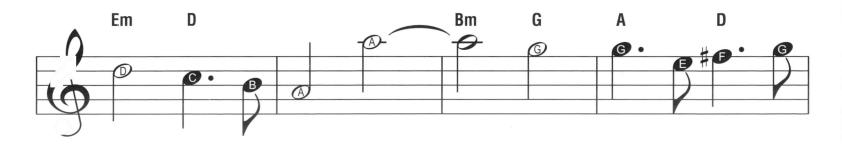

Alleluia

from Exsultate, jubilate

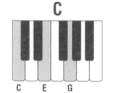
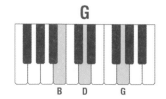
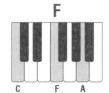
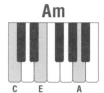
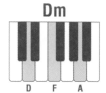

By Wolfgang Amadeus Mozart

Moderately fast

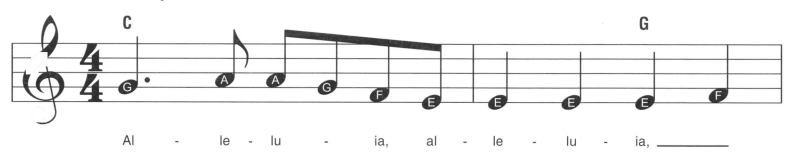

Al - le - lu - ia, al - le - lu - ia, _____

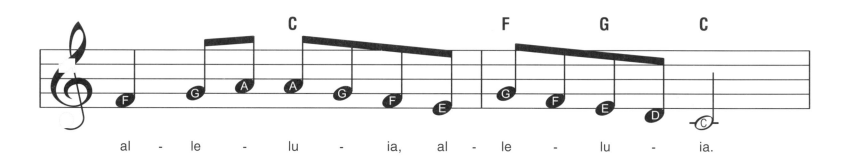

al - le - lu - ia, al - le - lu - ia.

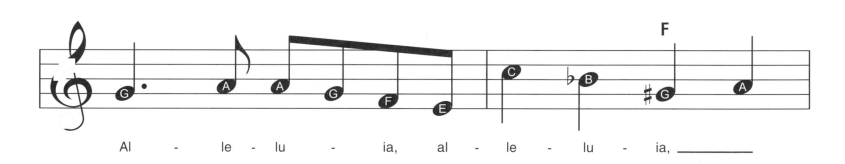

Al - le - lu - ia, al - le - lu - ia, _____

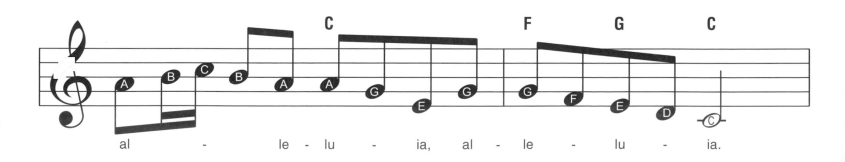

al - le - lu - ia, al - le - lu - ia.

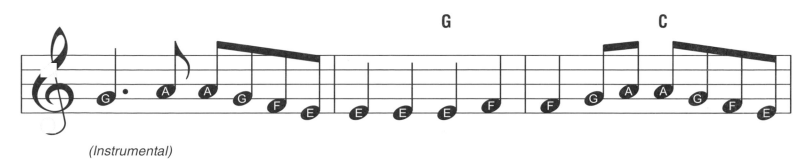

(Instrumental)

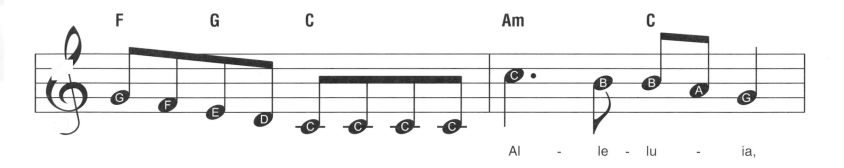

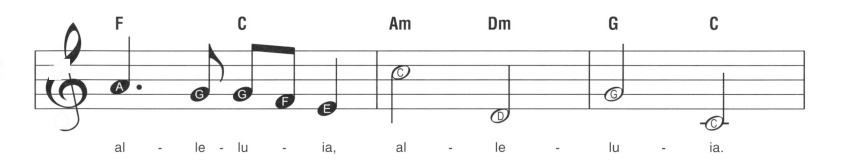

Al - le - lu - ia,

al - le - lu - ia, al - le - lu - ia.

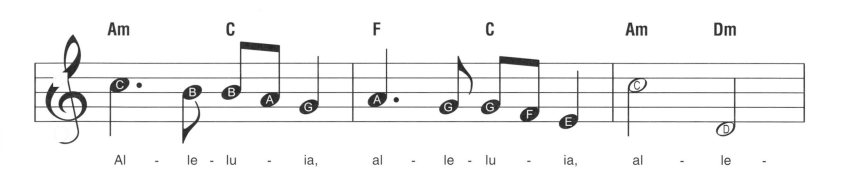

Al - le - lu - ia, al - le - lu - ia, al - le -

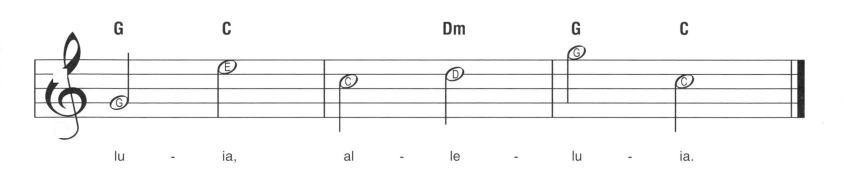

lu - ia, al - le - lu - ia.

Angel of Love

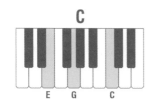

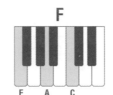
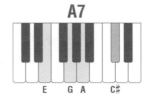
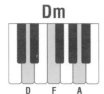

By Emil Waldteufel

Waltz tempo

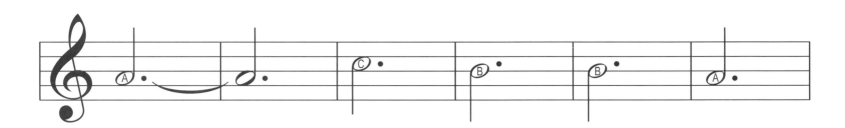

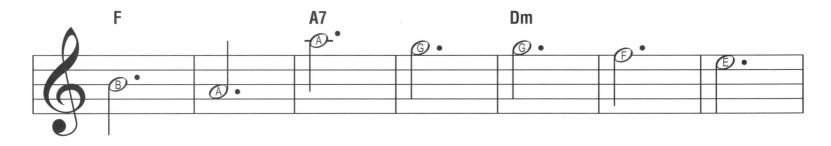

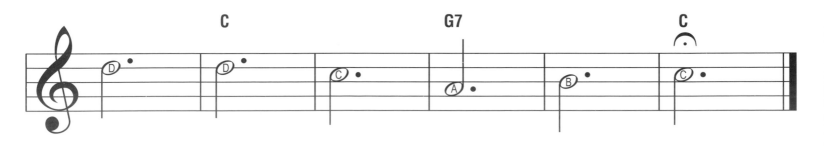

Bridal Chorus

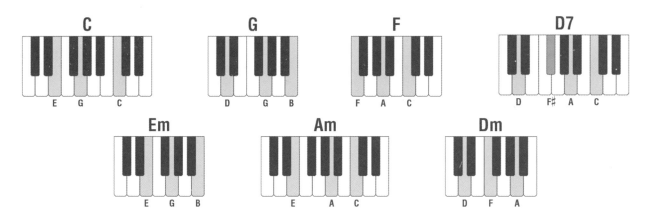

By Richard Wagner

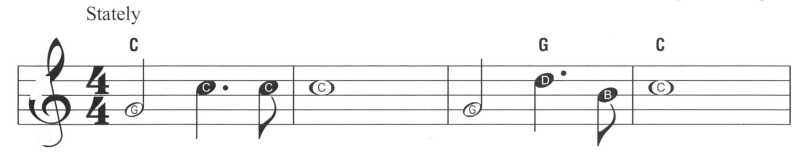

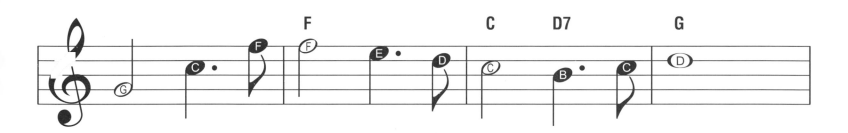

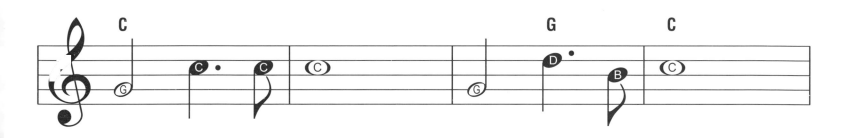

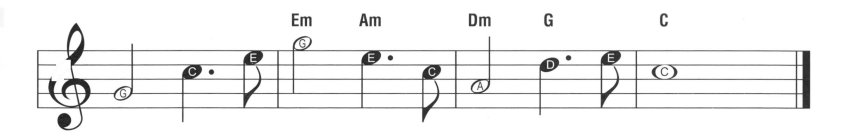

Arioso

By Johann Sebastian Bach

Berceuse

from Jocelyn

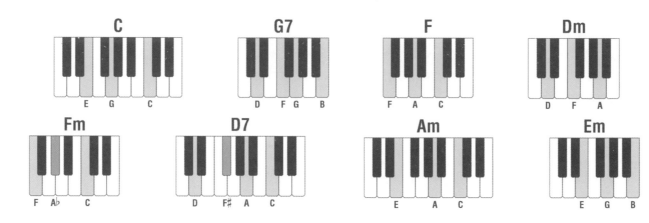

By Benjamin Godard

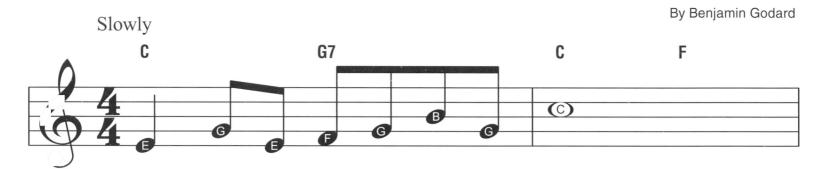

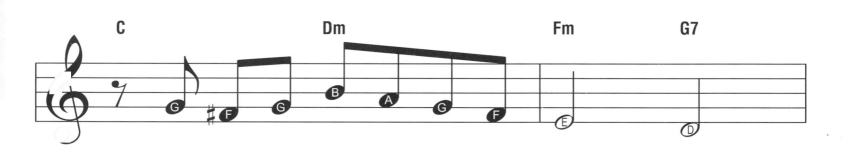

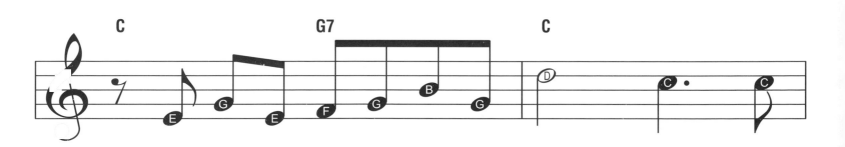

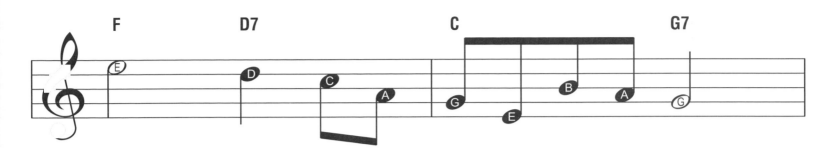

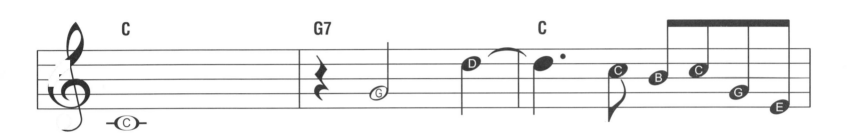

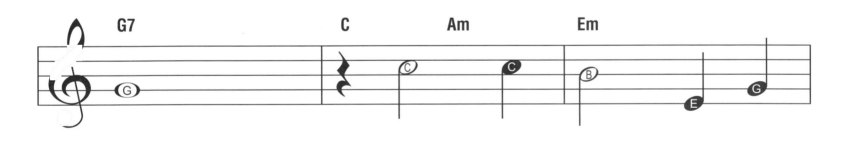

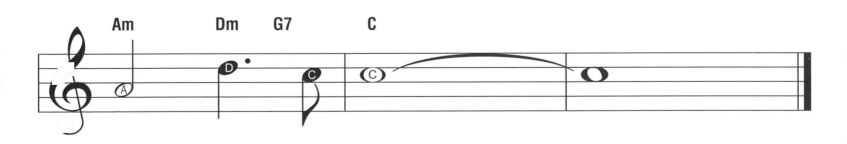

Bourée

from Suite for Lute

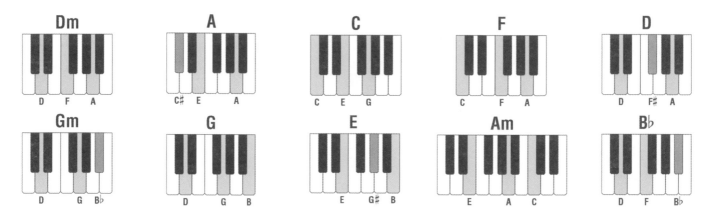

By Johann Sebastian Bach

Moderately fast

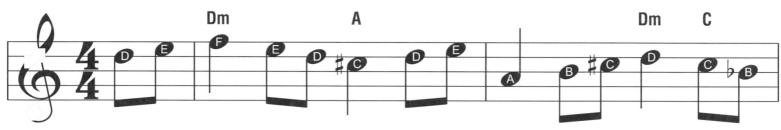

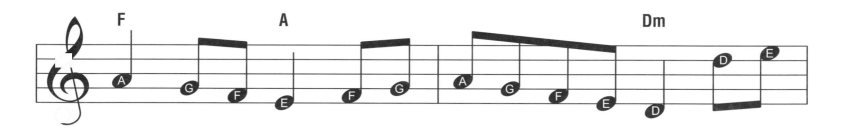

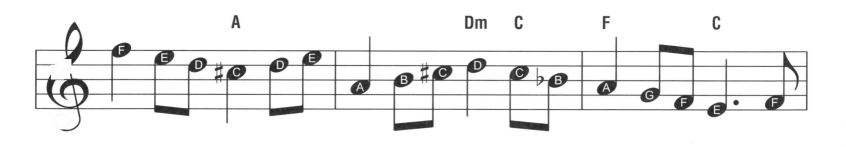

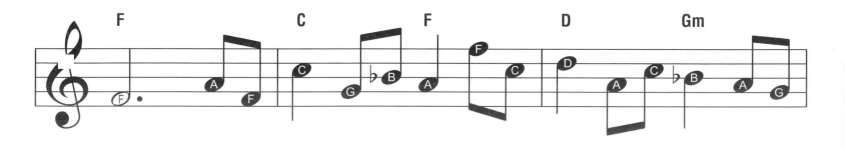

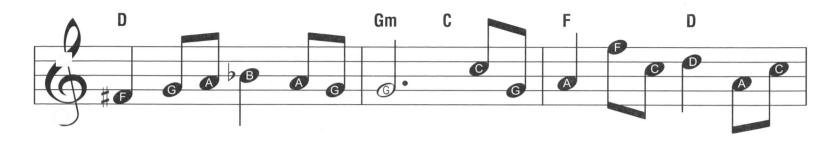

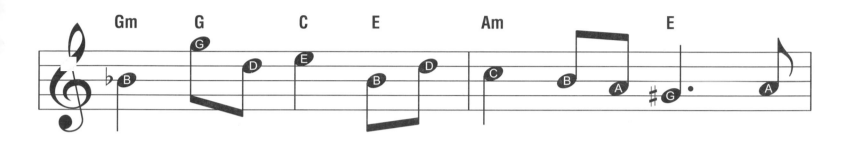

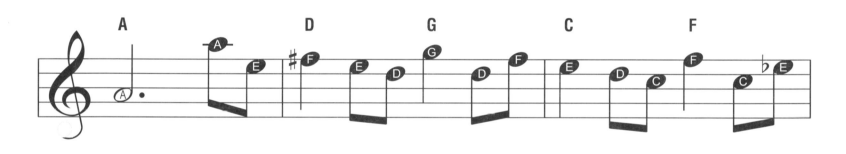

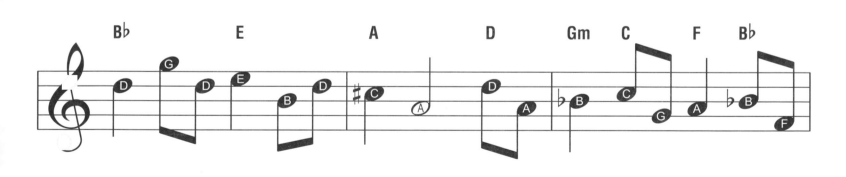

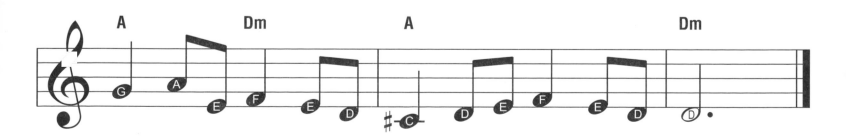

Can Can
from Orpheus in the Underworld

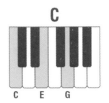 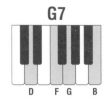 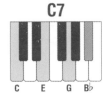 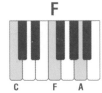 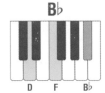

By Jacques Offenbach

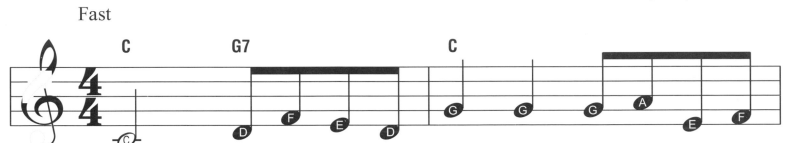

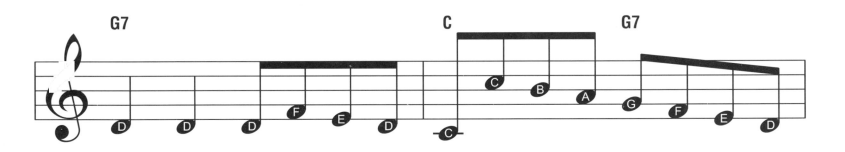

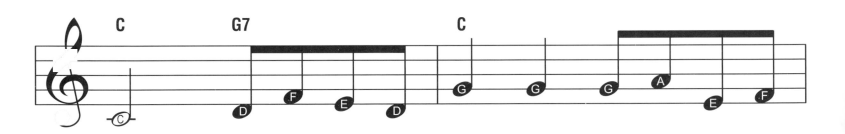

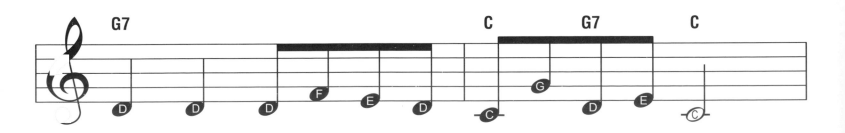

Canon

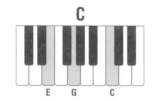
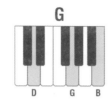
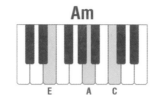
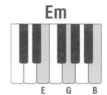
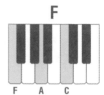

By Johann Pachelbel

Moderately slow

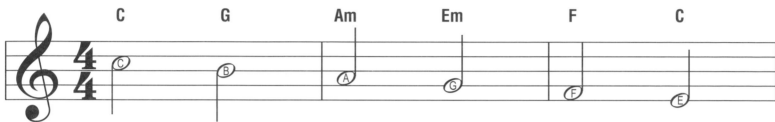

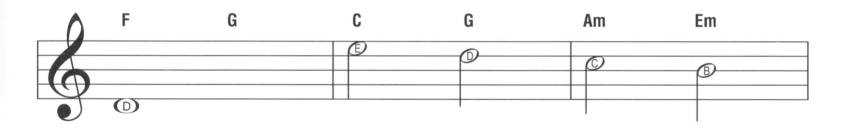

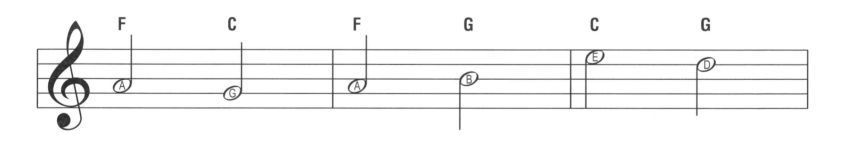

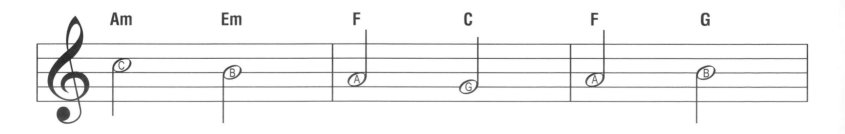

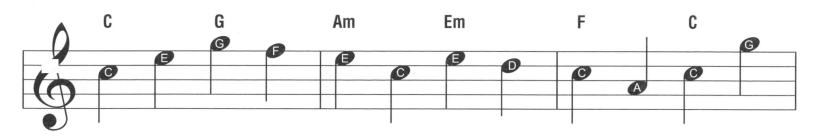

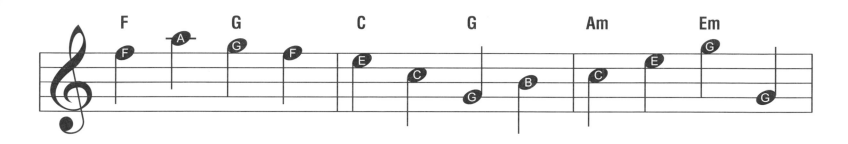

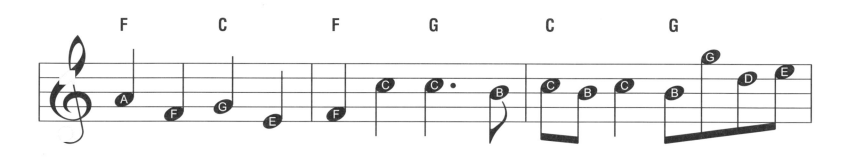

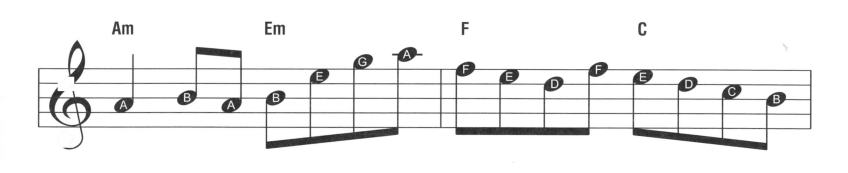

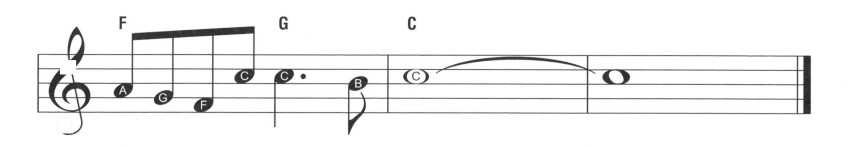

Carnival of Venice

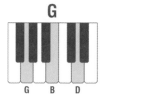

By Julius Benedict

With a lilt

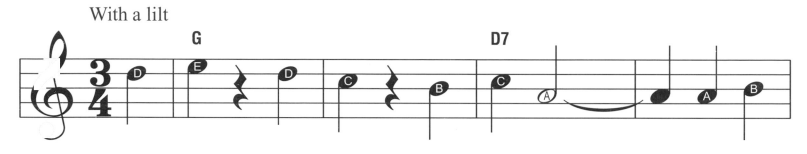

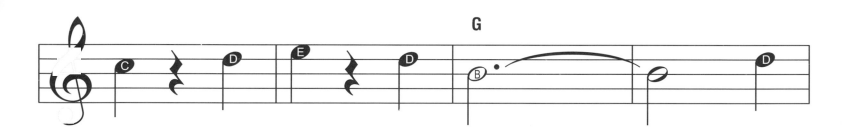

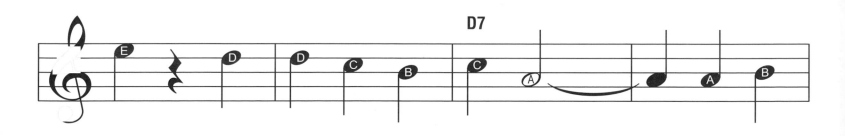

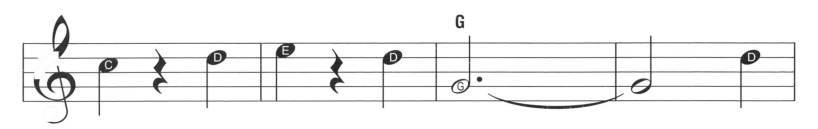

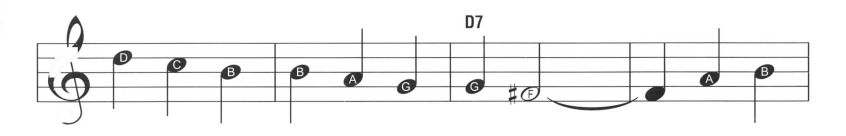

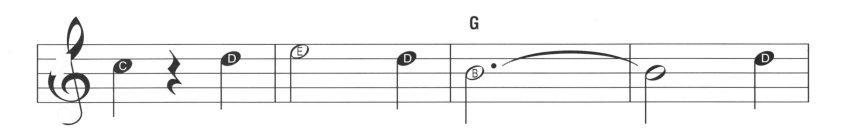

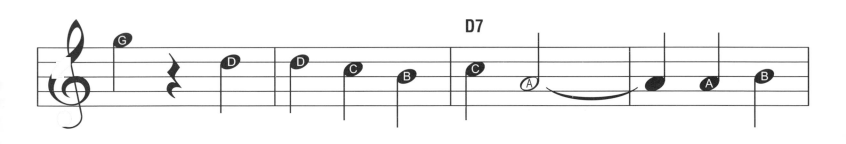

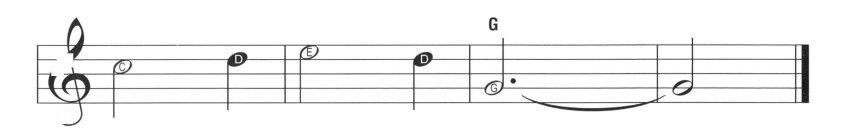

Choral Fantasy, Op. 80

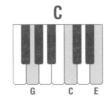
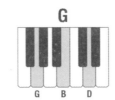
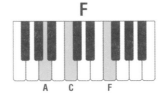

By Ludwig van Beethoven

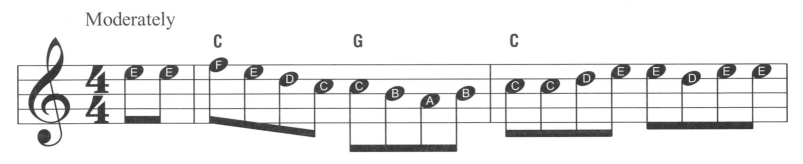

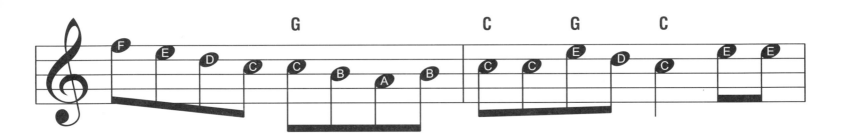

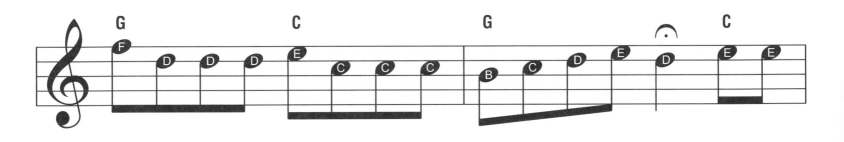

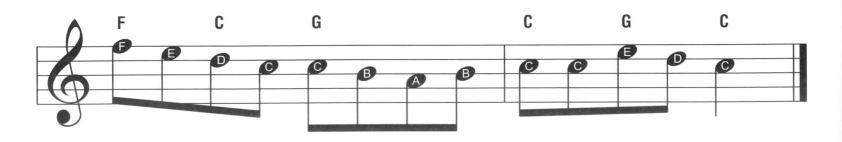

German Dance

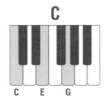
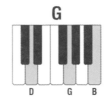
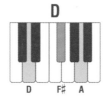

By Wolfgang Amadeus Mozart

Cielito Lindo

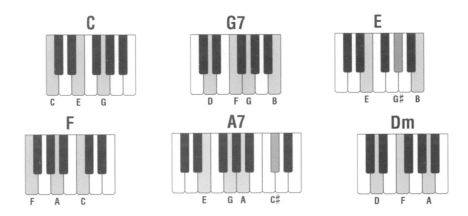

By C. Fernandez

Moderately fast

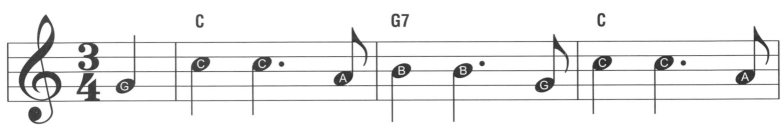

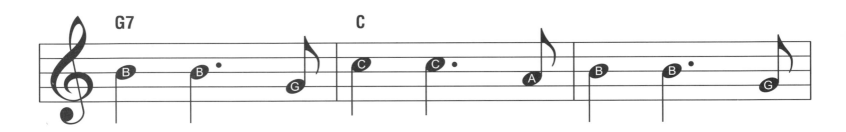

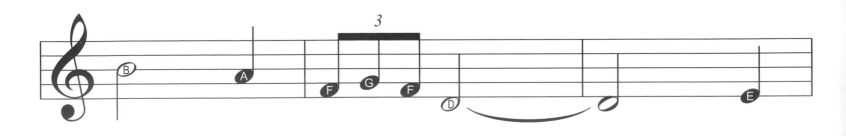

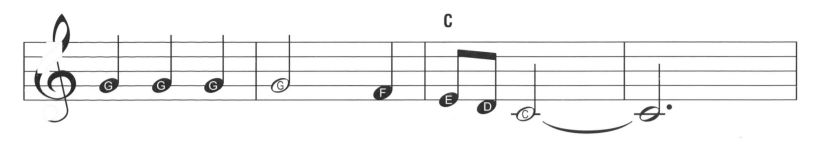

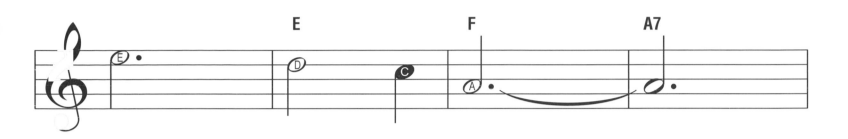

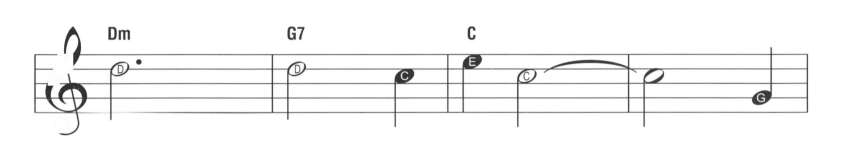

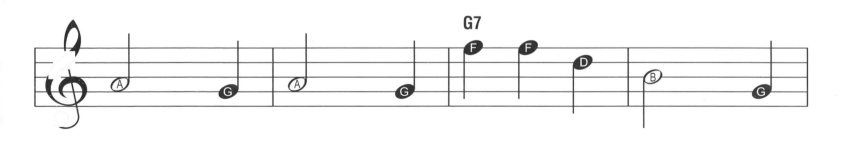

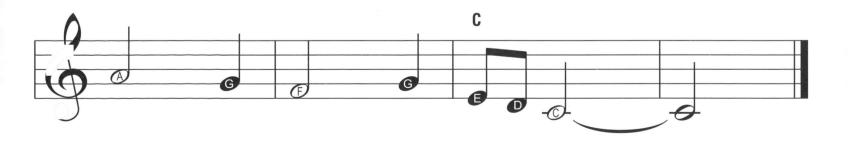

Danube Waves

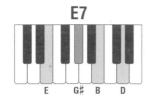
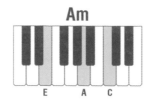
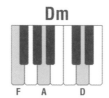

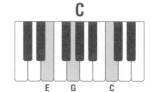

By Ion Ivanovici

Moderate Waltz

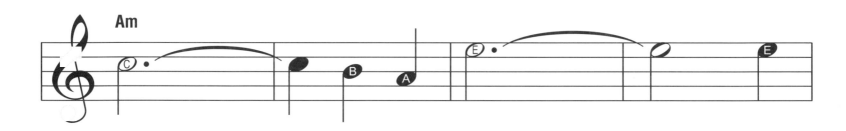

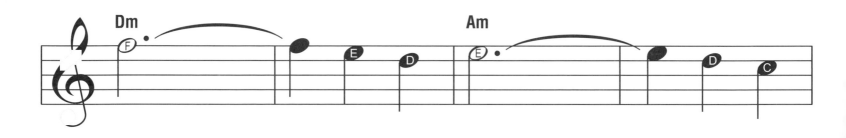

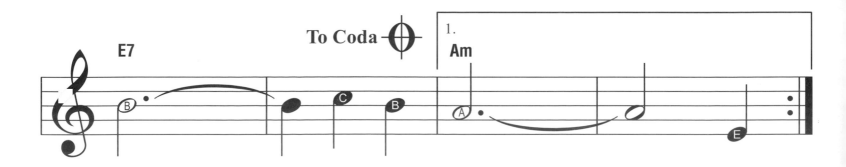

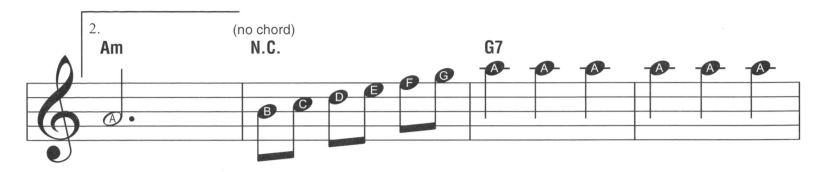

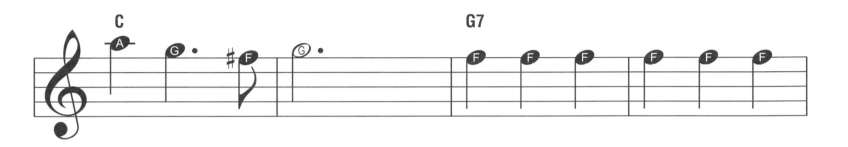

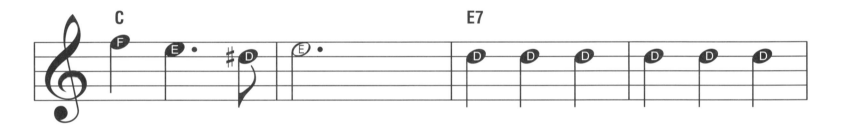

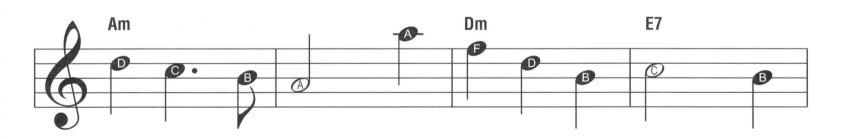

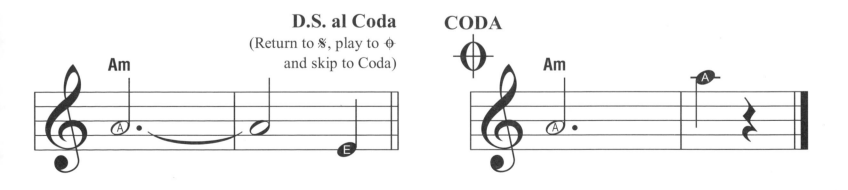

Dona Nobis Pacem

Canon

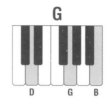
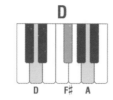
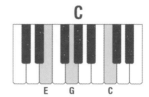

Traditional Canon

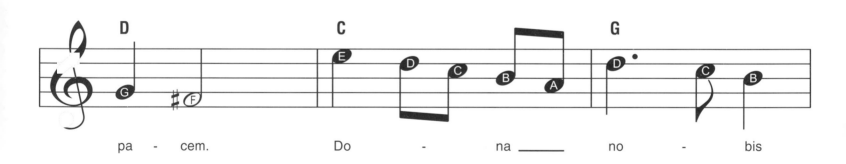

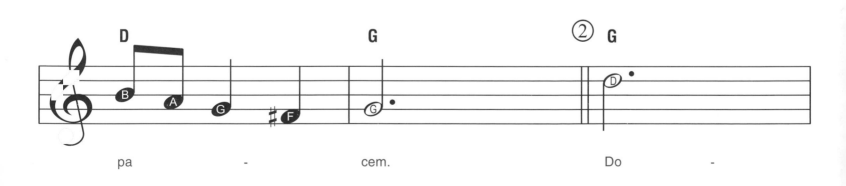

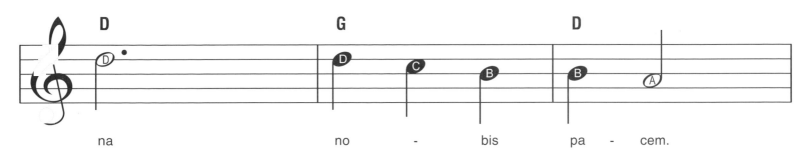

na no - bis pa - cem.

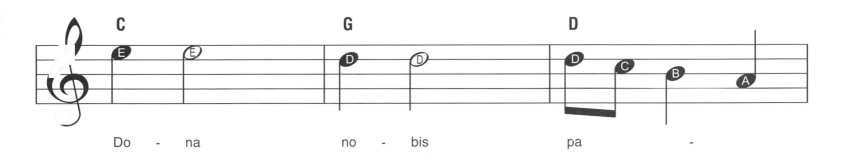

Do - na no - bis pa -

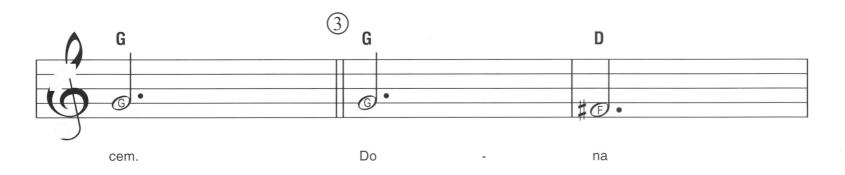

cem. Do - na

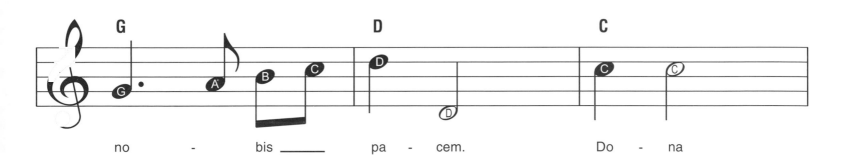

no - bis _____ pa - cem. Do - na

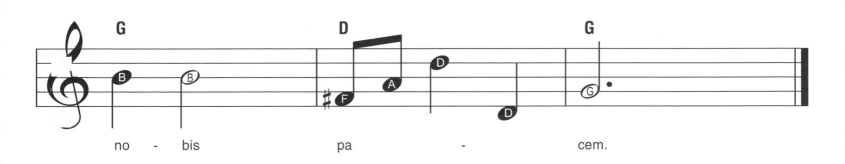

no - bis pa - cem.

Emperor Waltz

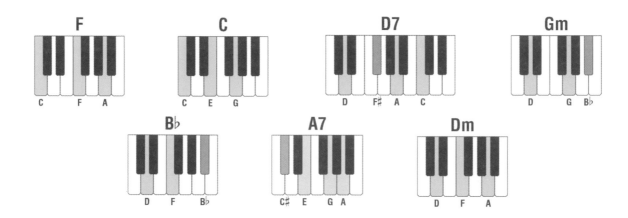

By Johann Strauss, Jr.

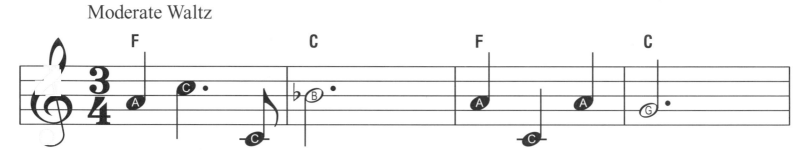

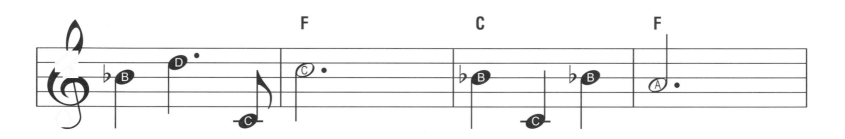

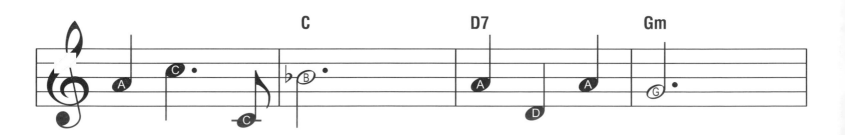

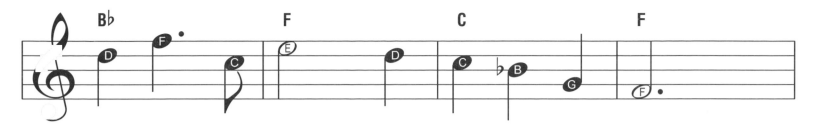

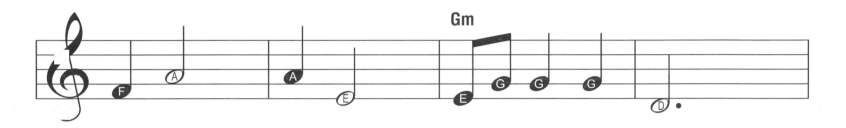

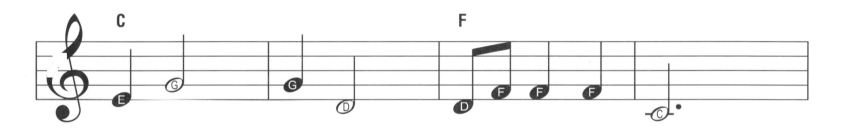

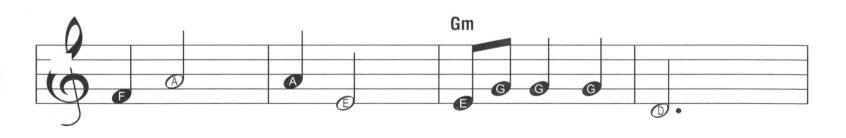

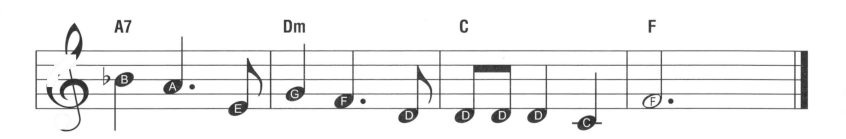

Farandole

from L'Arlésienne

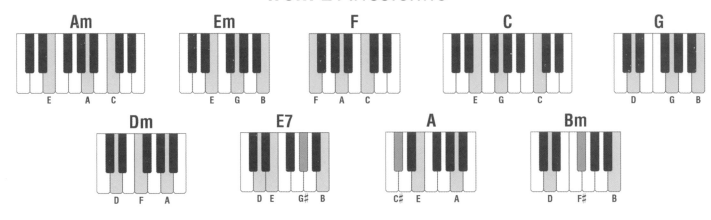

By Georges Bizet

Quickly

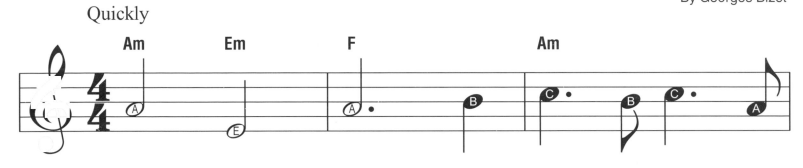

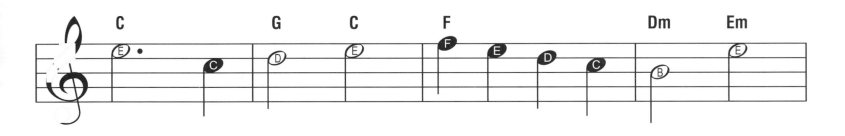

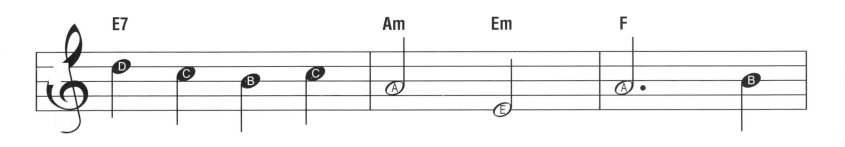

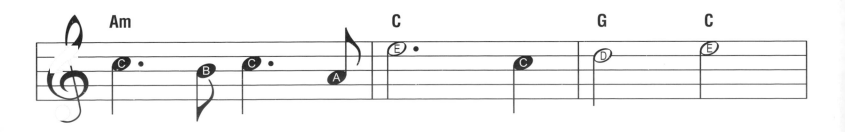

Funeral March

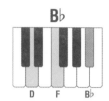
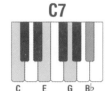
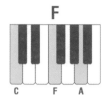
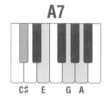

By Frédéric Chopin

Slowly

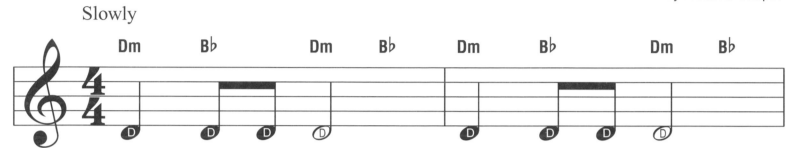

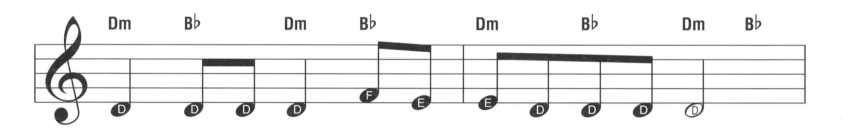

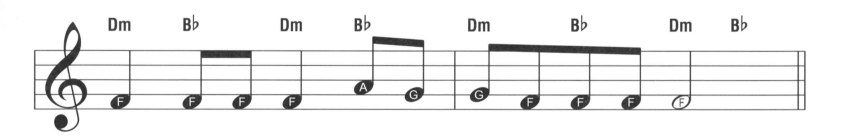

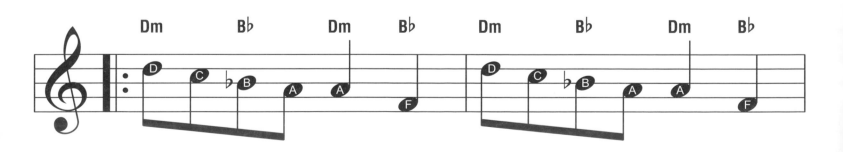

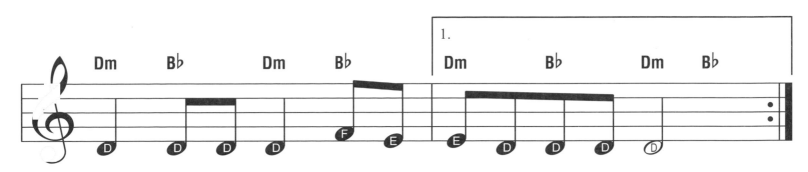

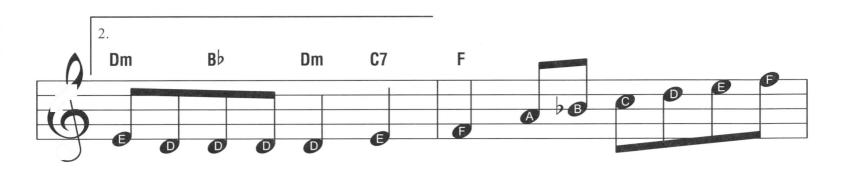

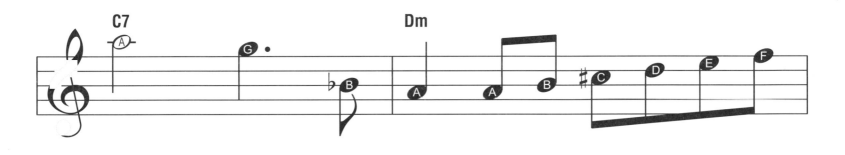

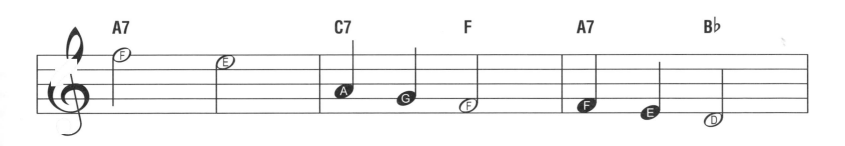

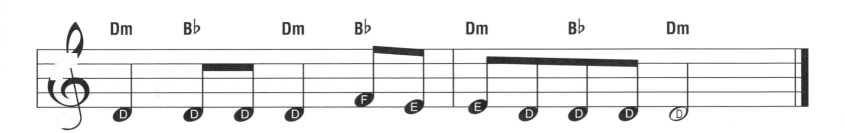

Funeral March of a Marionette

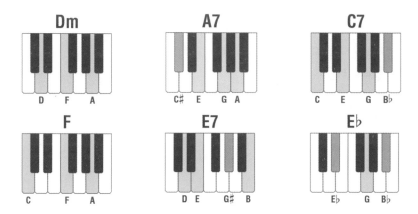

By Charles Gounod

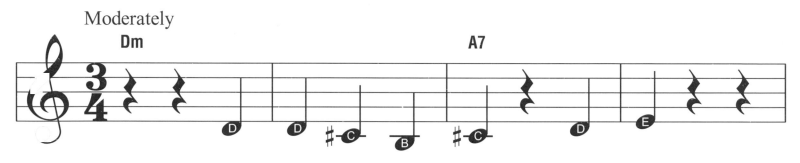

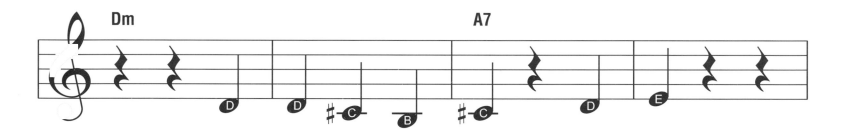

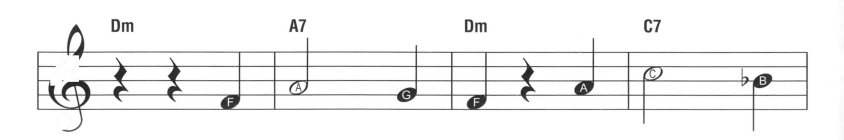

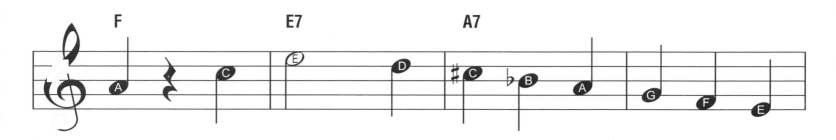

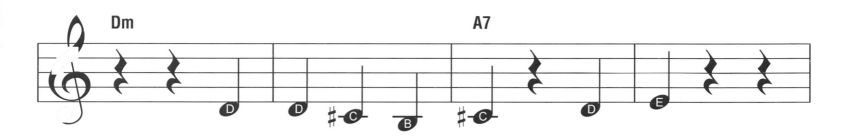

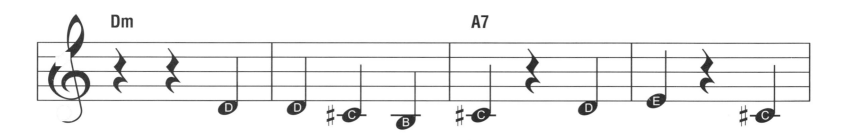

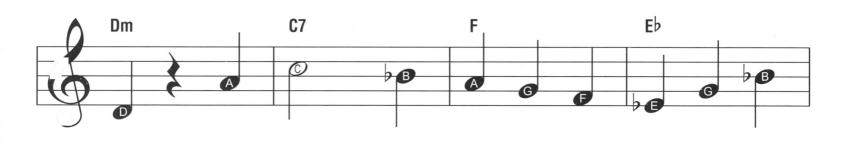

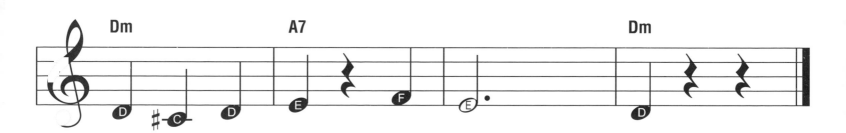

Für Elise

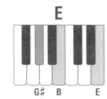
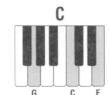

By Ludwig van Beethoven

Moderately, with motion
(no chord)

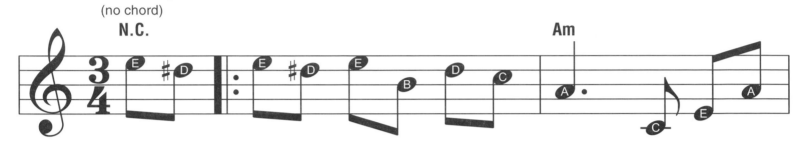

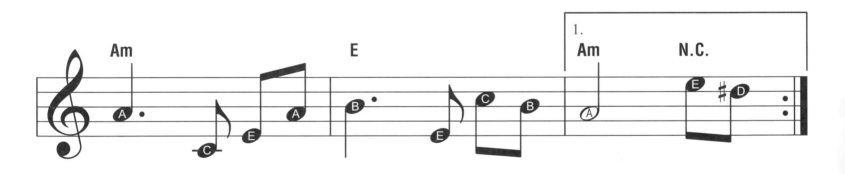

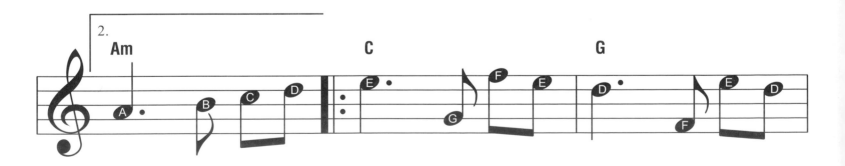

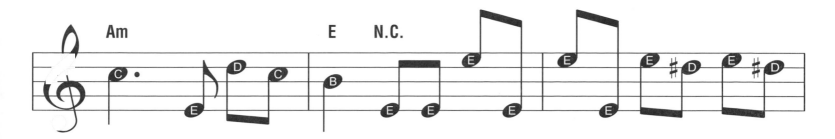

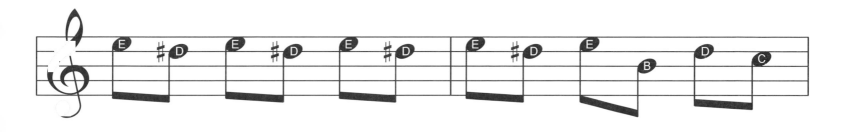

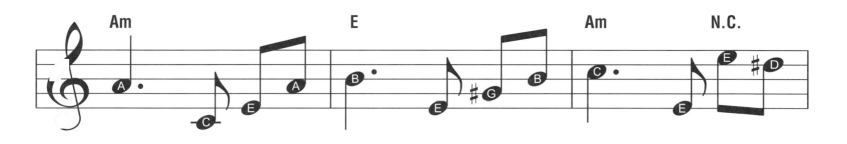

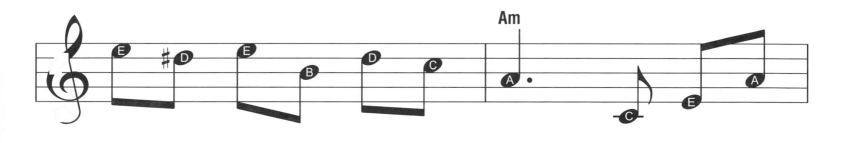

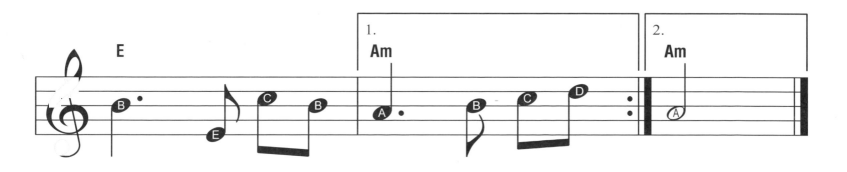

German National Anthem

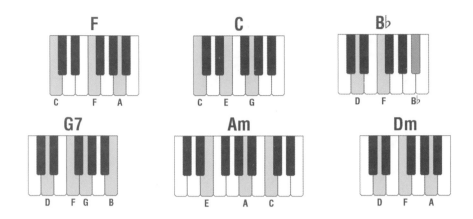

By Franz Joseph Haydn

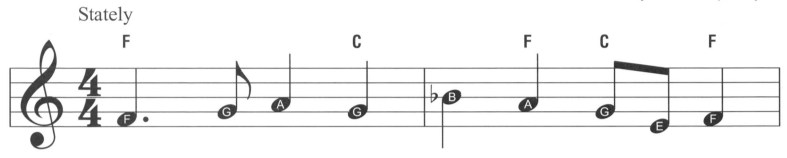

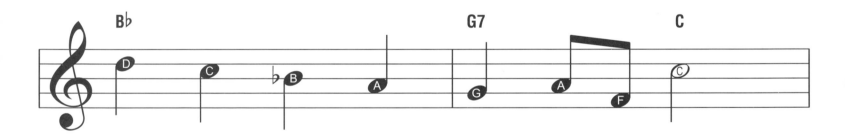

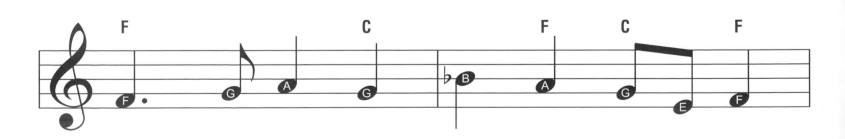

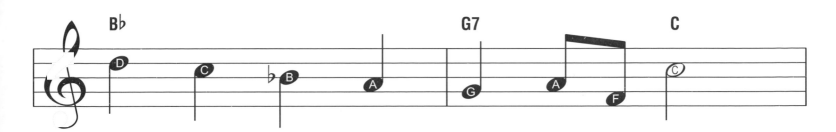

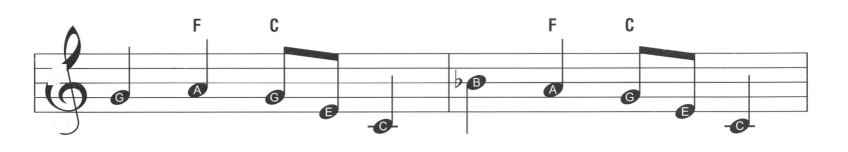

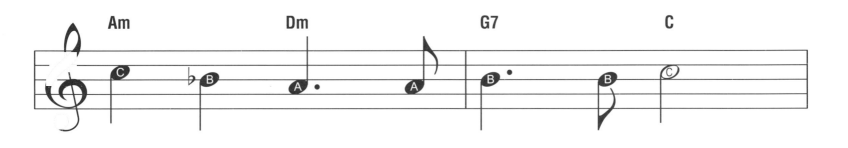

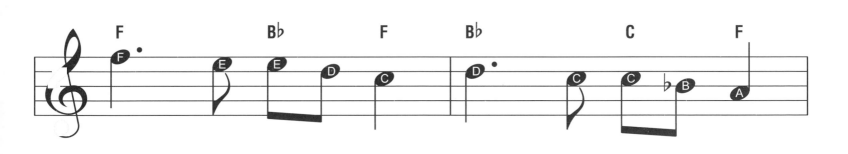

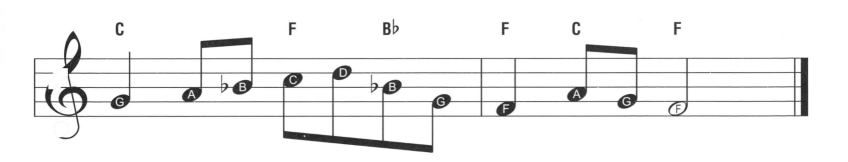

The Happy Farmer

from Album for the Young

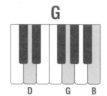
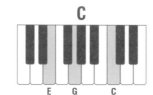
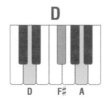
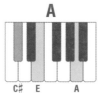

By Robert Schumann

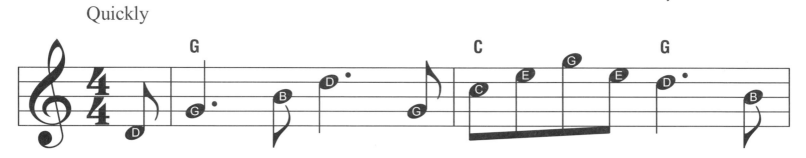

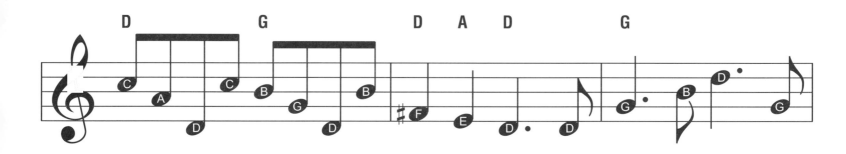

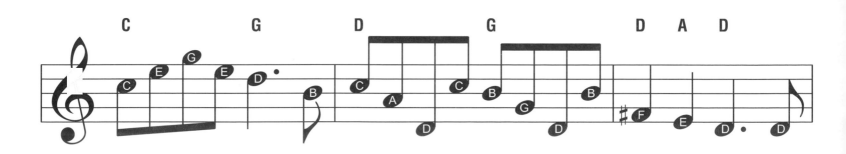

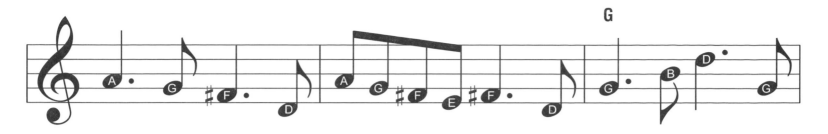

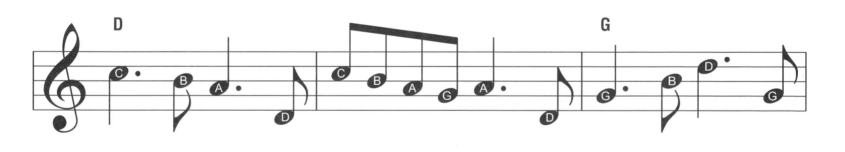

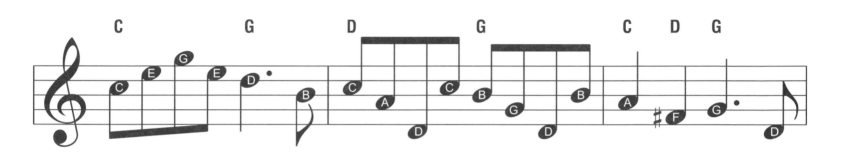

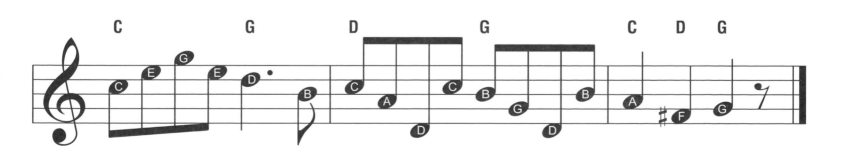

Hearts and Flowers

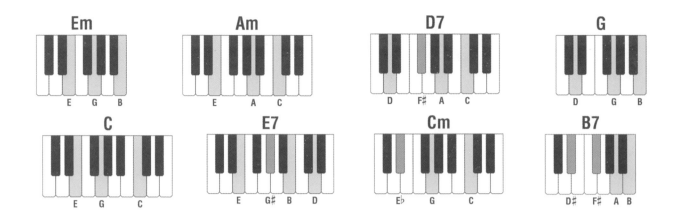

By Theodore M. Tobani

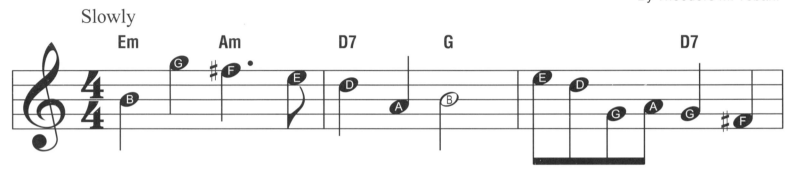

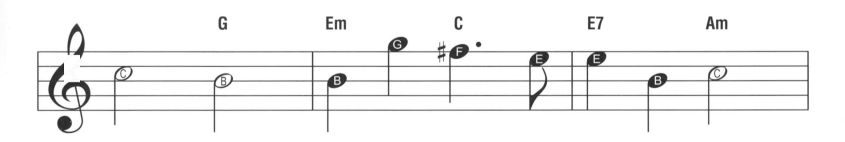

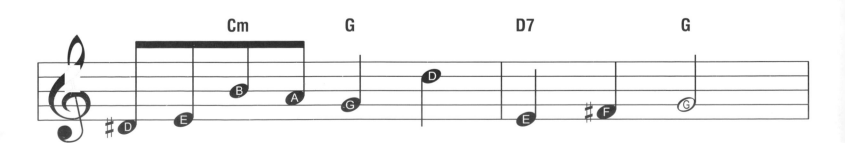

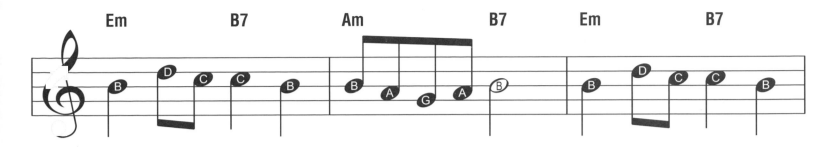

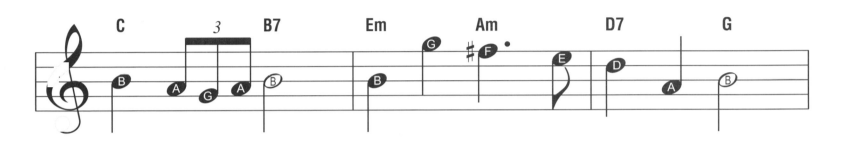

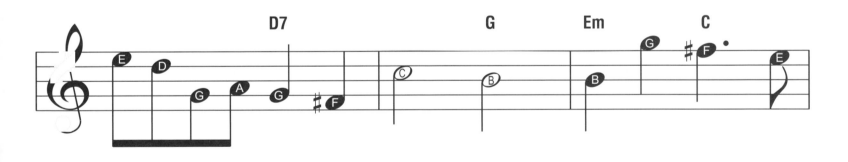

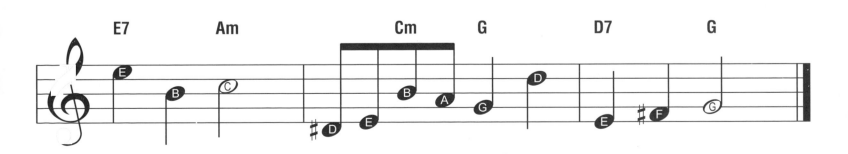

Humoresque

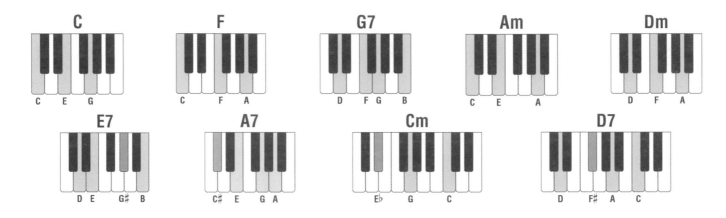

By Antonín Dvořák

Brightly, with a lilt

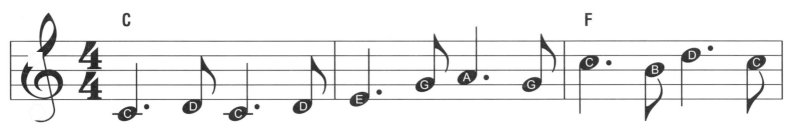

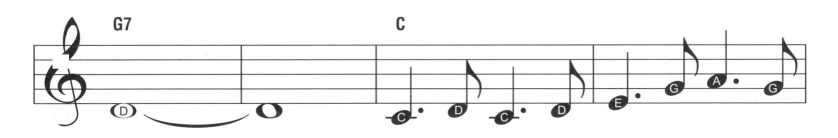

To Coda ⊕

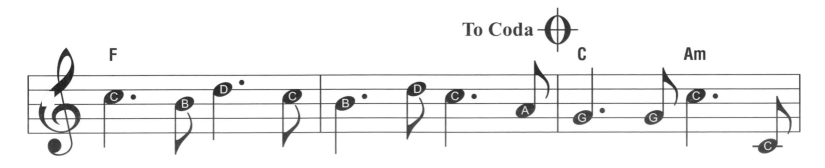

D.C. al Coda
(Return to beginning,
play to ⊕ and skip to Coda)

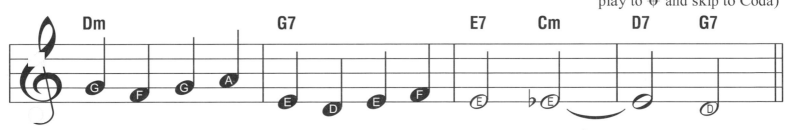

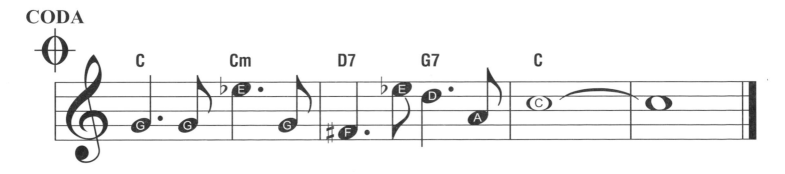

Impromptu, Op. 142, No. 2

By Franz Schubert

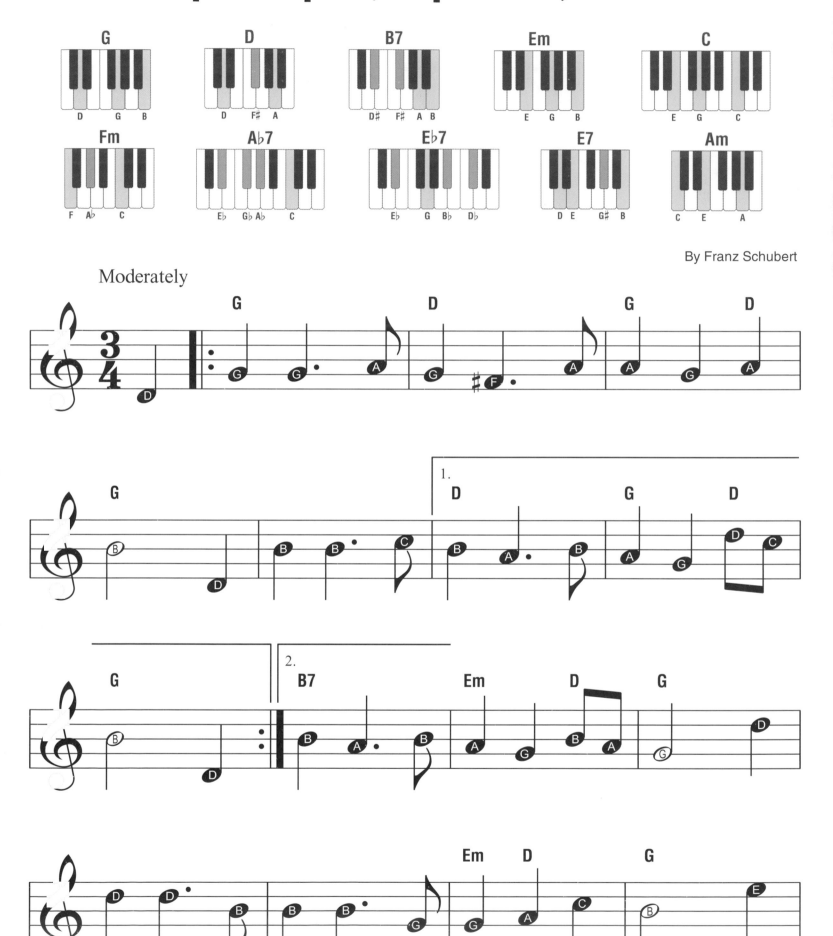

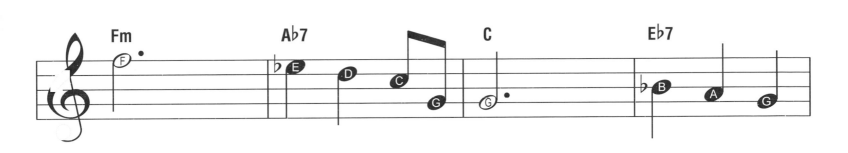

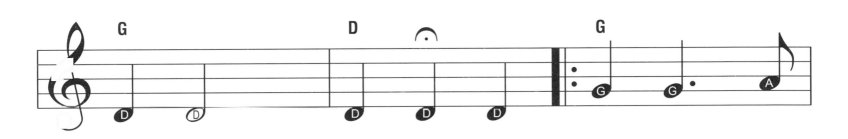

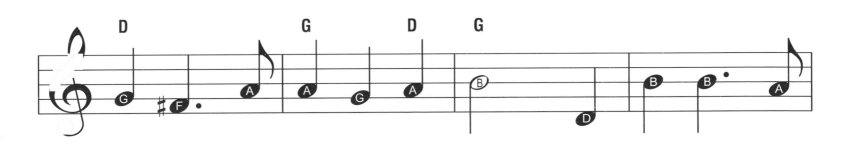

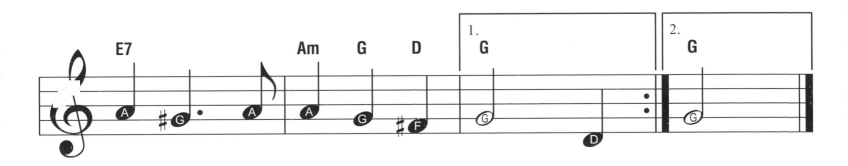

Jesu, Joy of Man's Desiring

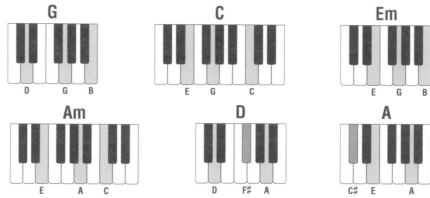

By Johann Sebastian Bach

Flowing

(continue triplet rhythm)

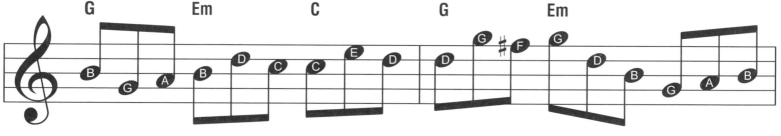

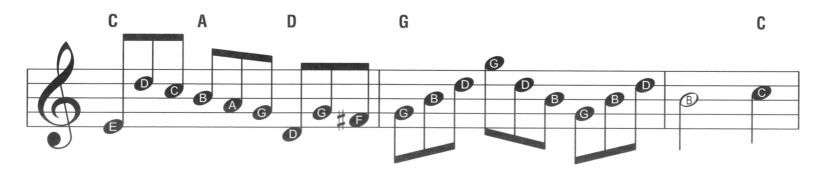

Jupiter
Chorale Theme from The Planets

By Gustav Holst

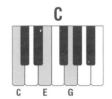
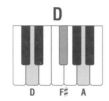
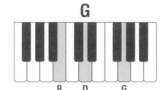
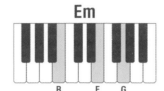
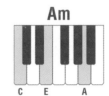

Majestically

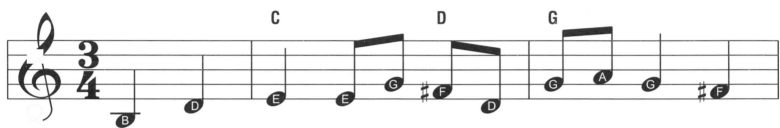

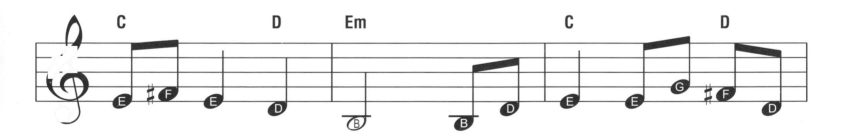

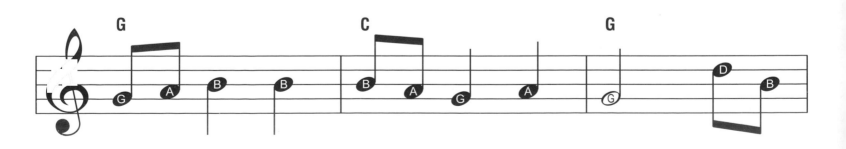

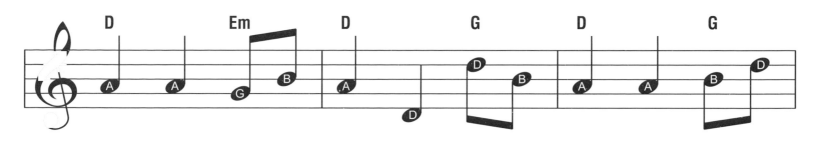

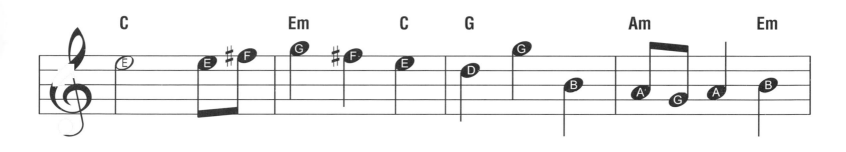

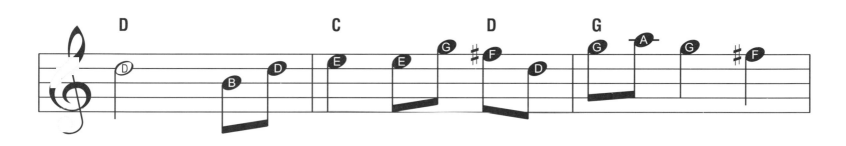

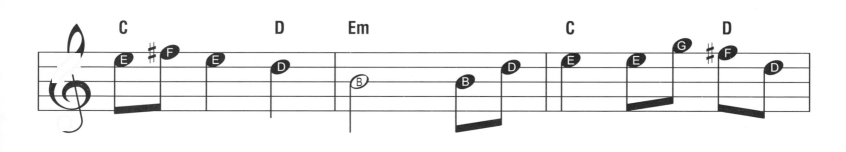

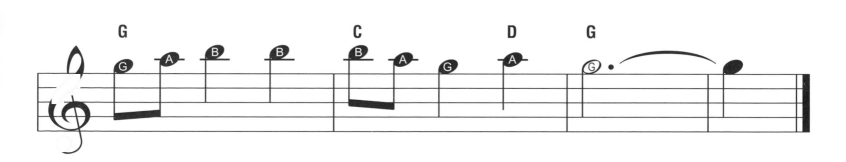

Lullaby

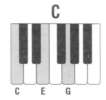
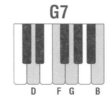

By Johannes Brahms

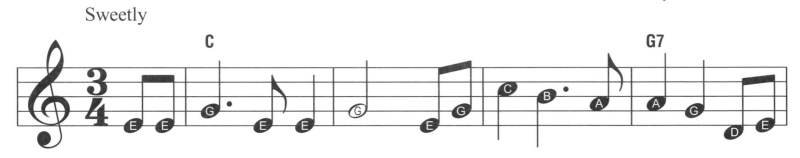

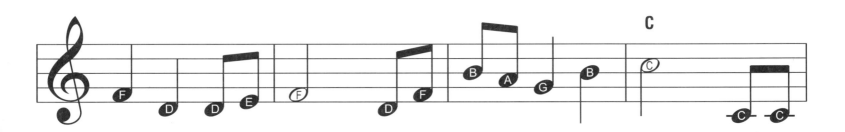

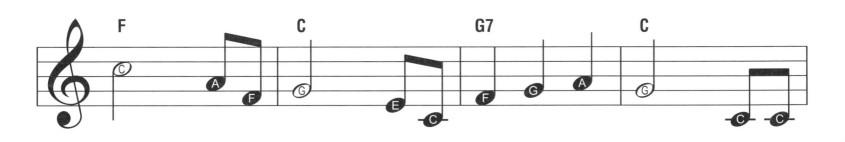

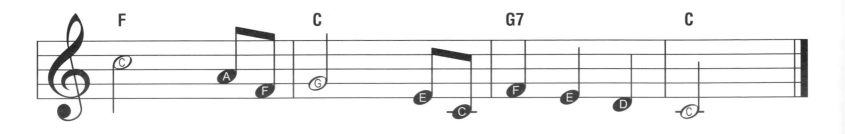

Prelude, Op. 28, No. 7

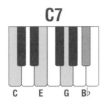
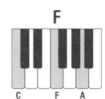
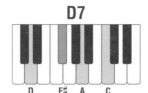

By Frédéric Chopin

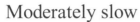

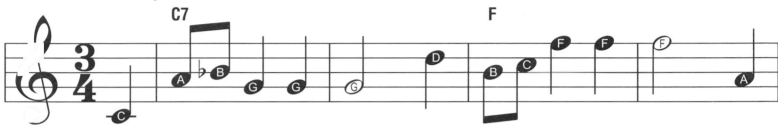

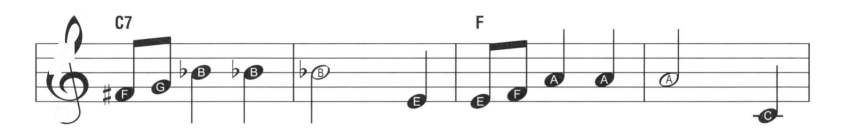

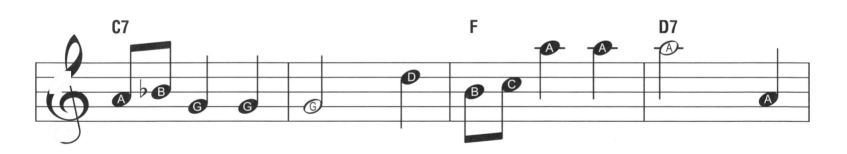

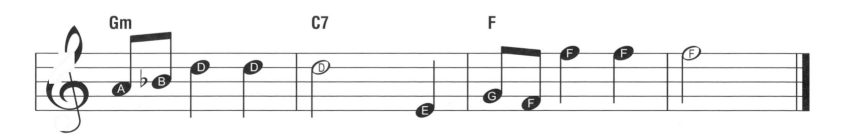

Melody

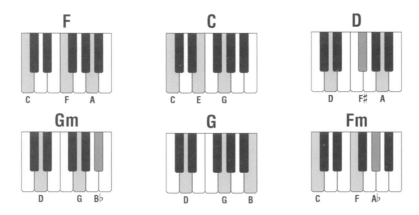

By Anton Rubinstein

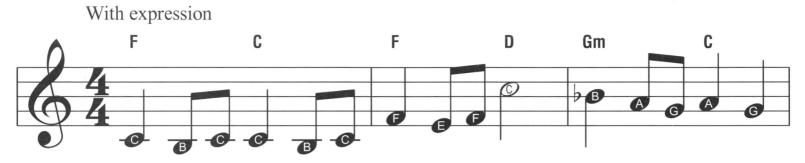

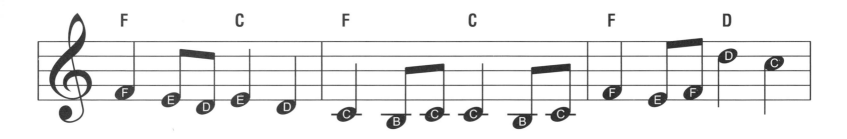

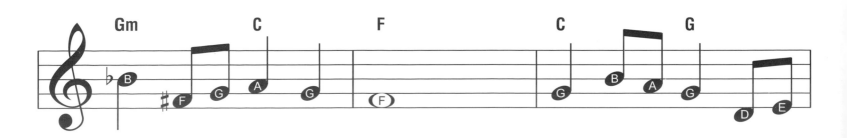

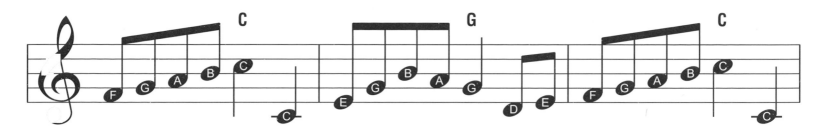

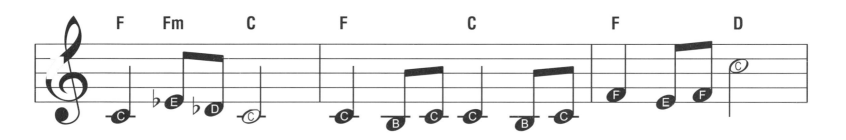

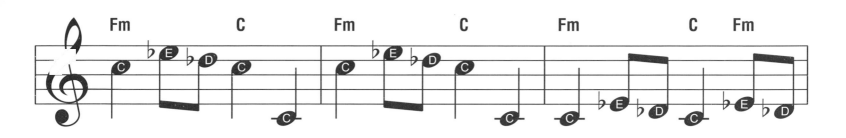

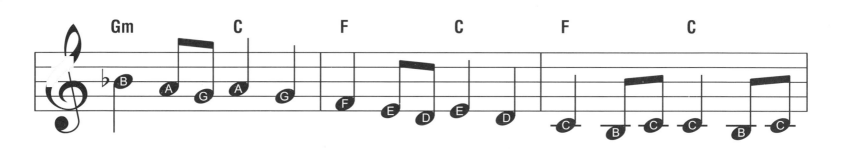

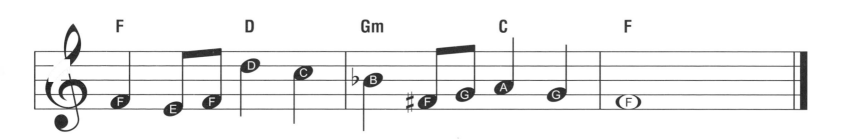

The Merry Widow Waltz

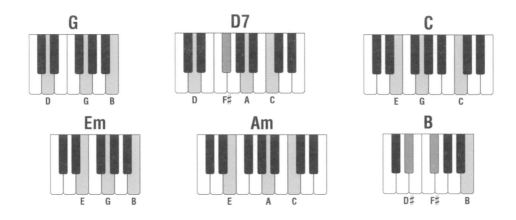

By Franz Lehár

Moderate Waltz

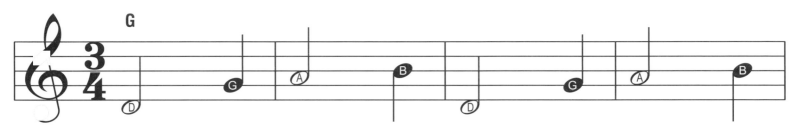

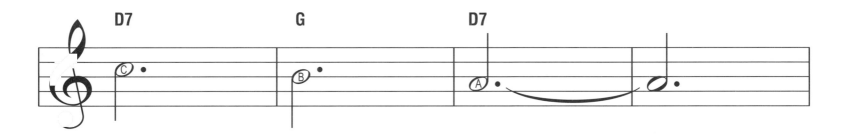

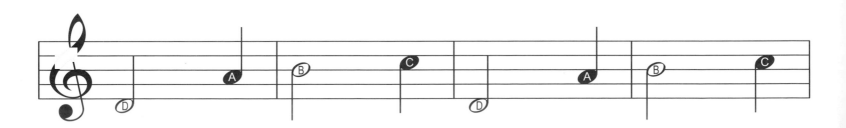

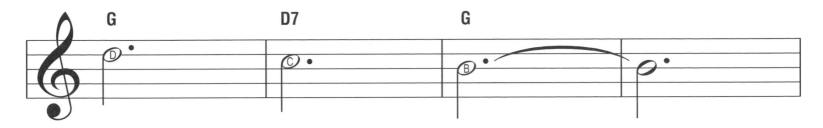

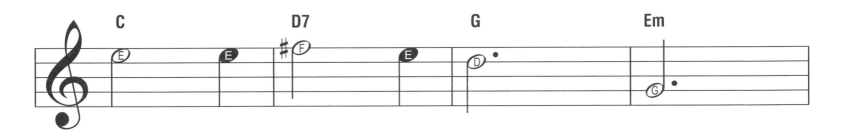

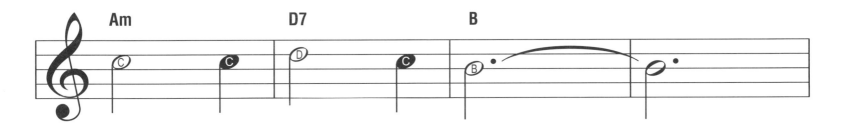

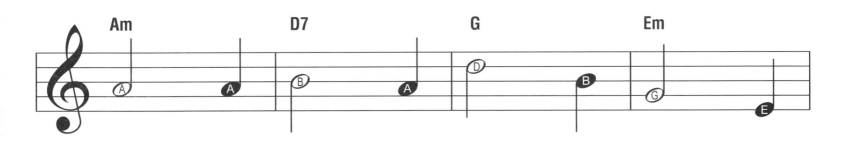

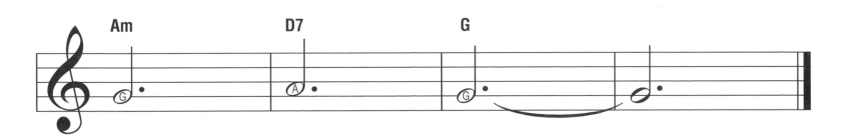

Minuet I

from The Anna Magdalena Notebook

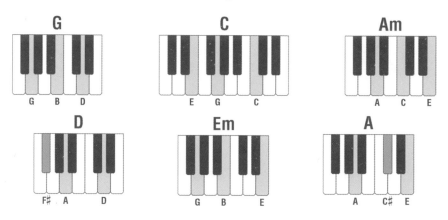

By Johann Sebastian Bach

Moderately fast

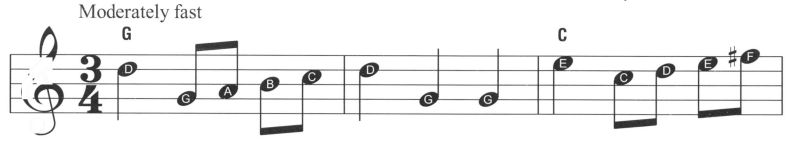

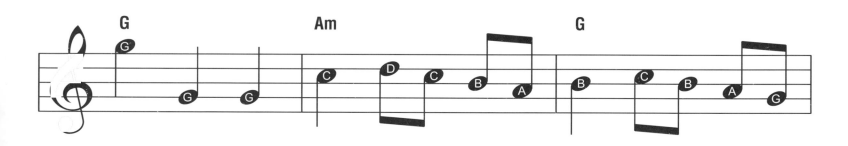

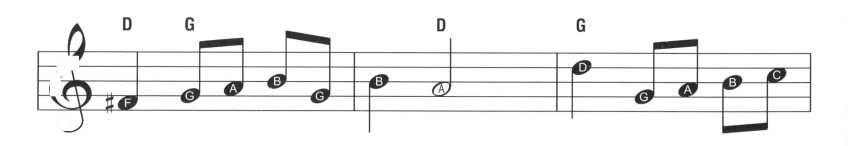

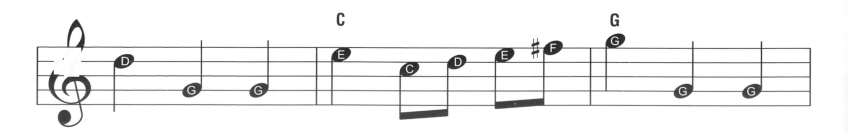

Minuet II

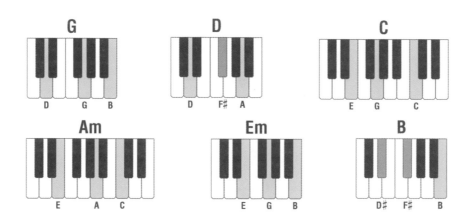

By Johann Sebastian Bach

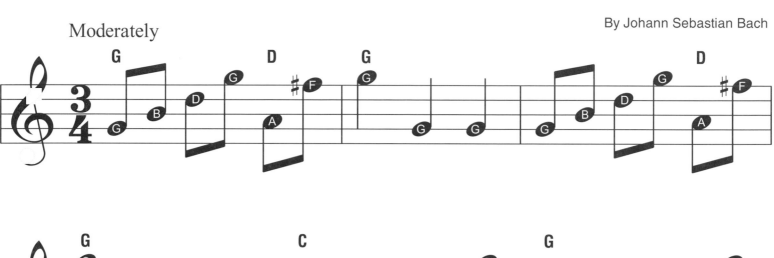

Moderately

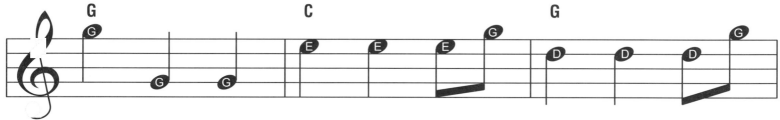

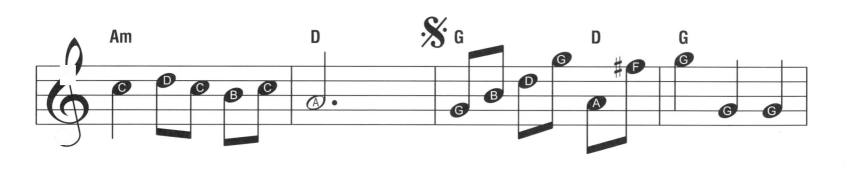

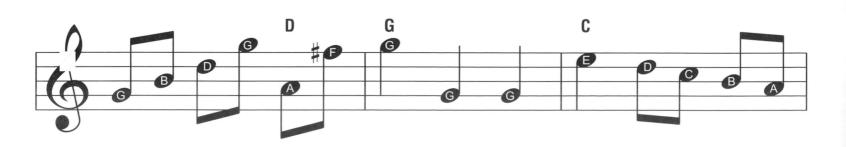

The Moldau

from *Má Vlast*

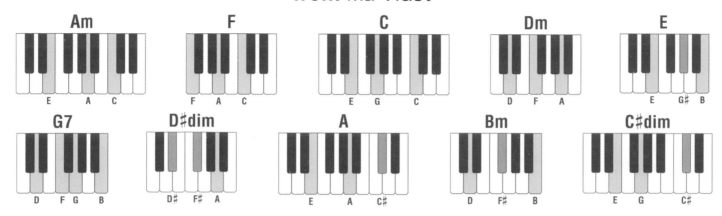

By Bedřich Smetana

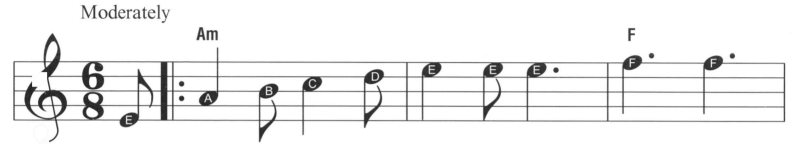

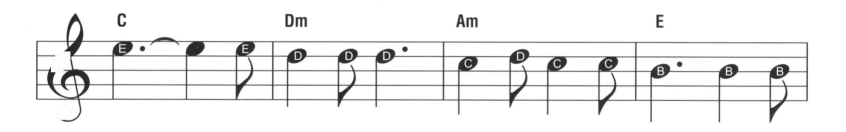

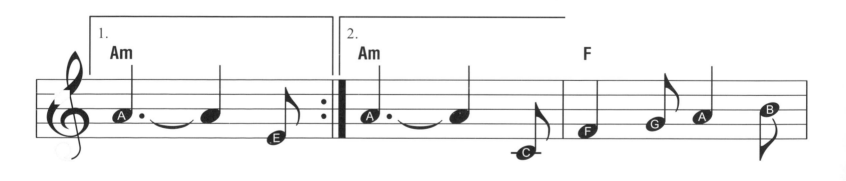

Musette

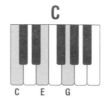
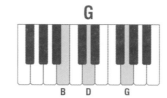
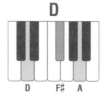

By Johann Sebastian Bach

Moderately

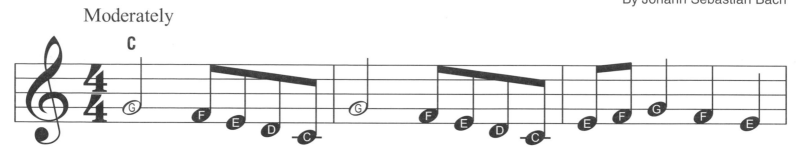

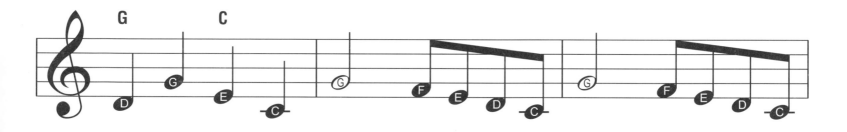

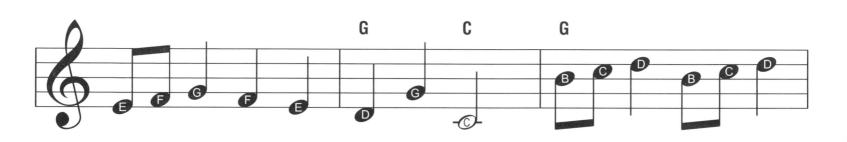

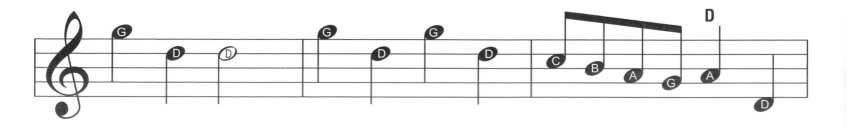

'O Sole Mio

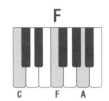
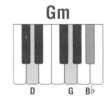
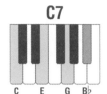
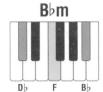

By E. Di Capua

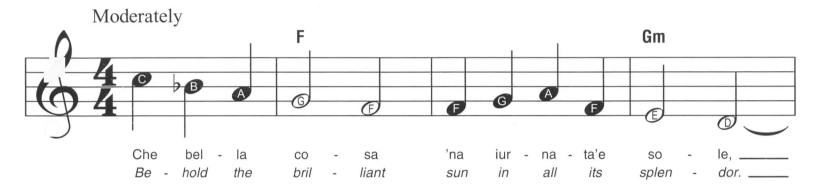

Che bel - la co - sa 'na iur - na - ta'e so - le, _____
Be - hold the bril - liant sun in all its splen - dor. _____

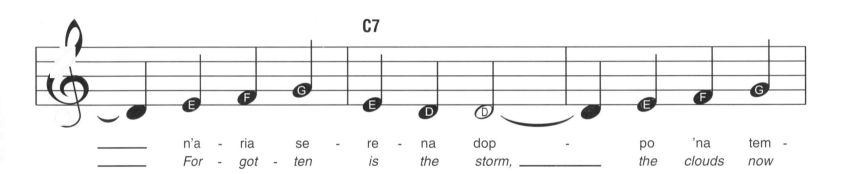

_____ n'a - ria se - re - na dop - po 'na tem -
_____ For - got - ten is the storm, _____ the clouds now

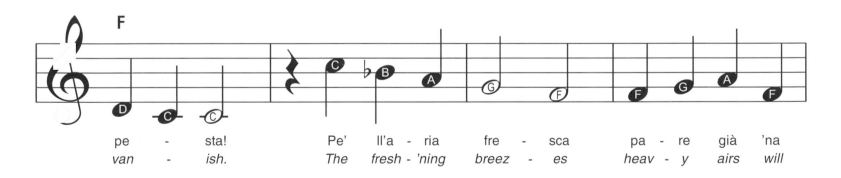

pe - sta! Pe' ll'a - ria fre - sca pa - re già 'na
van - ish. The fresh -'ning breez - es heav - y airs will

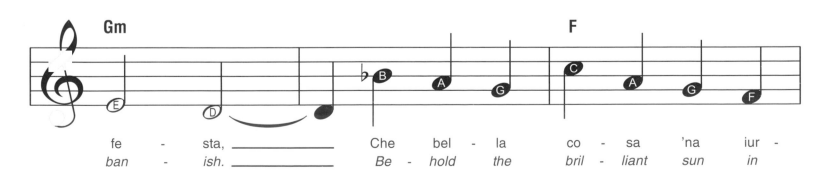

fe - sta, _____ Che bel - la co - sa 'na iur -
ban - ish. _____ Be - hold the bril - liant sun in

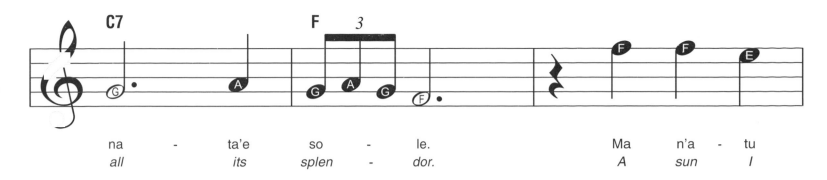

na - ta'e so - le.
all its splen - dor.
Ma n'a - tu
A sun I

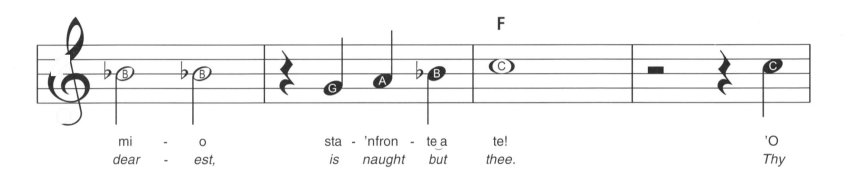

so - le cchiù bel - lo, ohi - ne',
know of that's bright - er still.
'o so - le
This sun, my

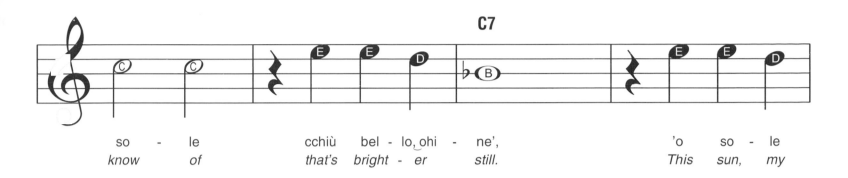

mi - o sta - 'nfron - te_a te!
dear - est, is naught but thee.
'O
Thy

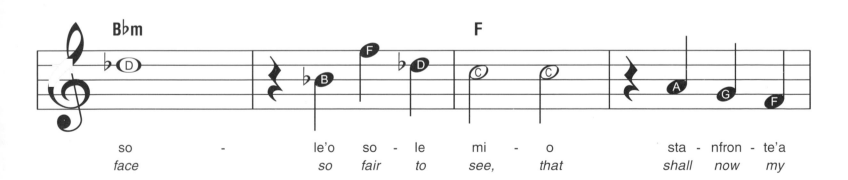

so - le'o so - le mi - o
face so fair to see, that
sta - nfron - te_a
shall now my

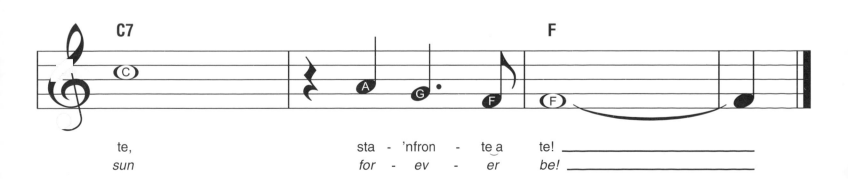

te, sta - 'nfron - te_a te! _____
sun for - ev - er be! _____

On the Beautiful Blue Danube

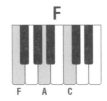
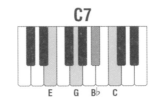
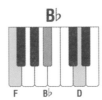

By Johann Strauss, Jr.

Moderate Waltz

(no chord)

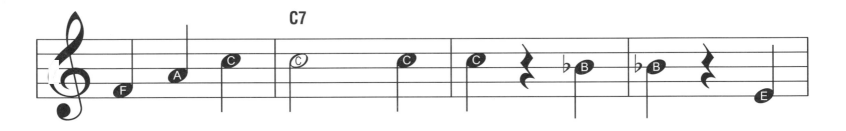

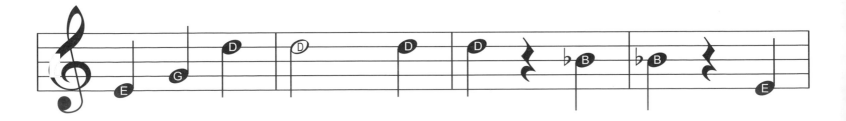

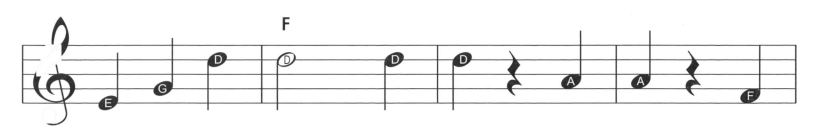

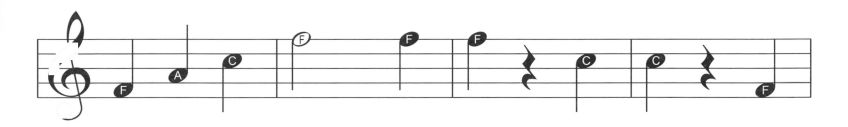

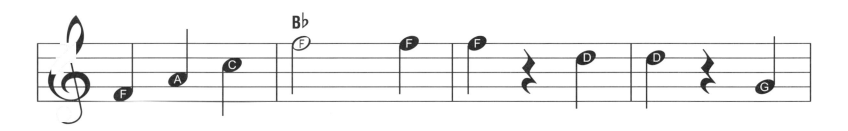

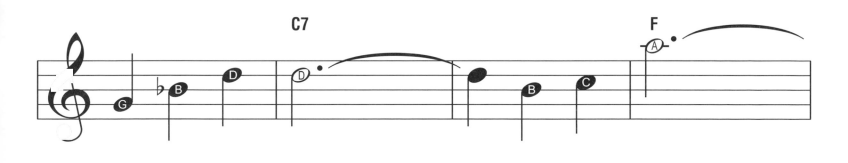

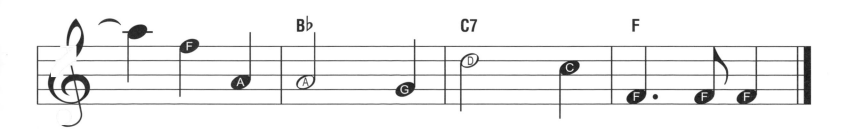

Over the Waves

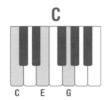
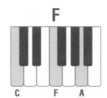

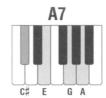
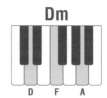

By Juventino Rosas

Moderate Waltz

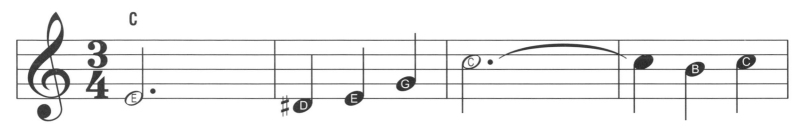

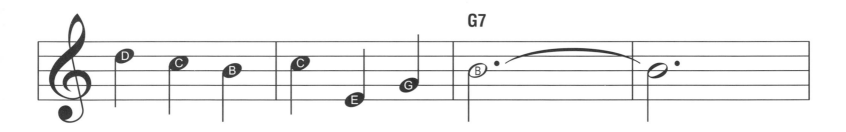

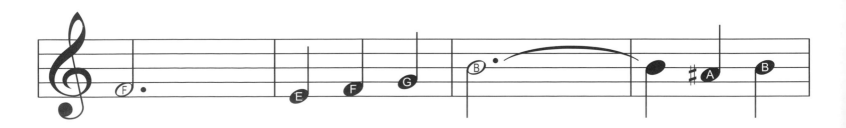

75

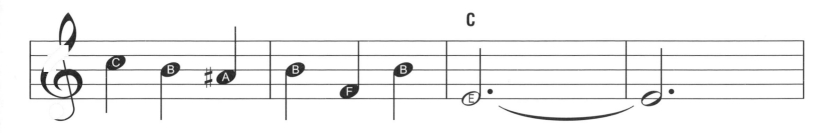

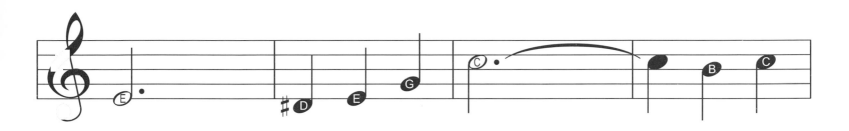

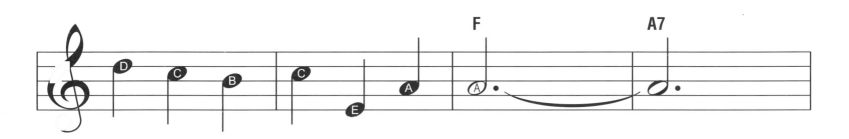

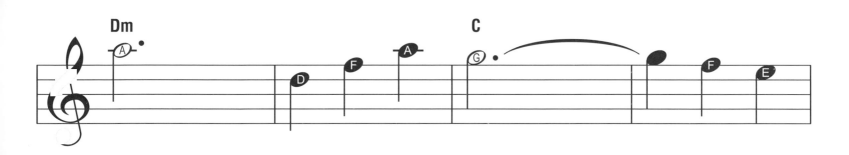

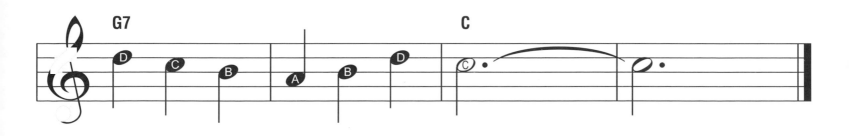

Piano Sonatina No. 1
First Movement Theme

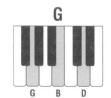
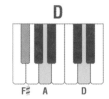
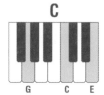

By Ludwig van Beethoven

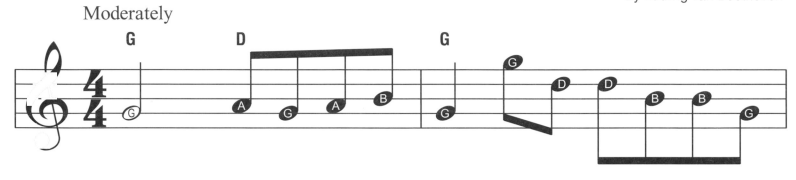

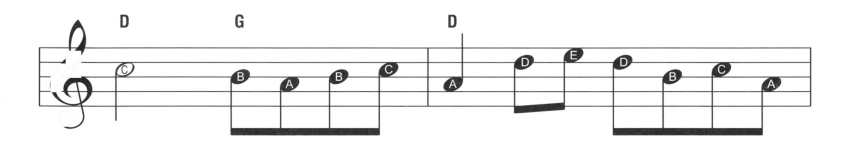

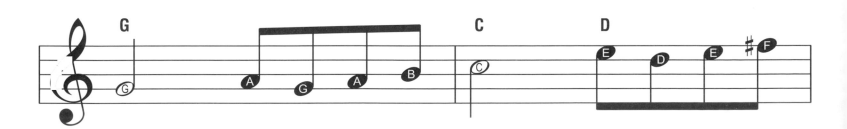

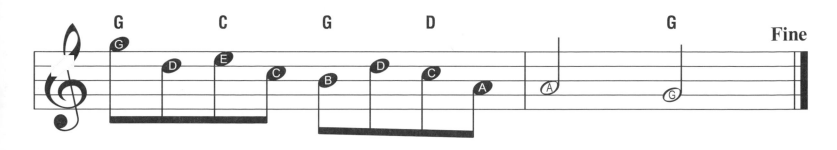

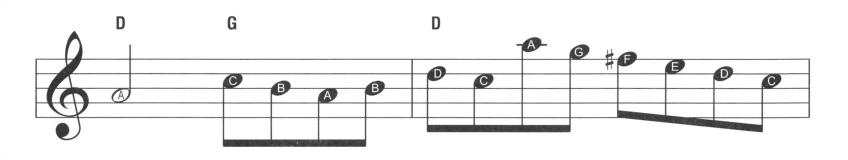

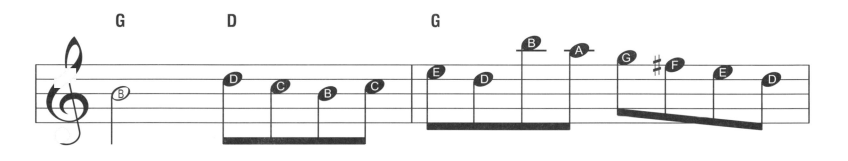

D.C. al Fine
(Return to beginning
and play to Fine)

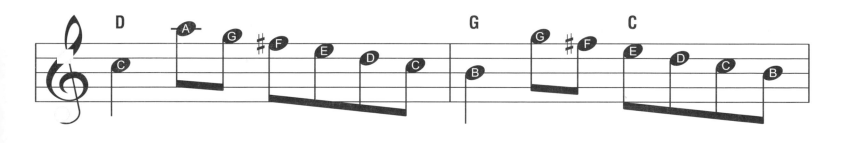

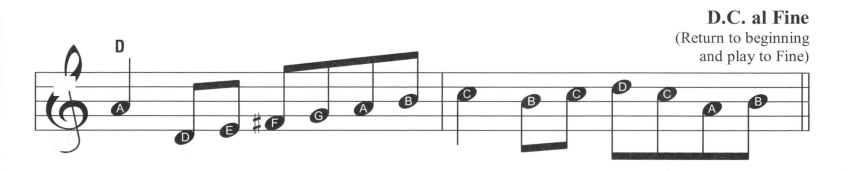

Pizzicato Polka

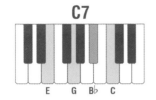
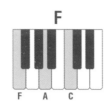
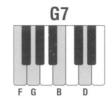
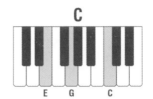
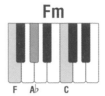

By Johann and Josef Strauss

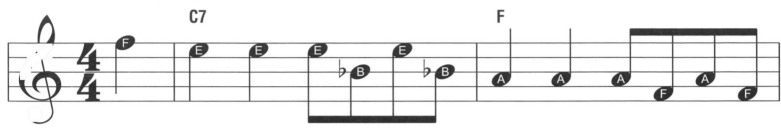

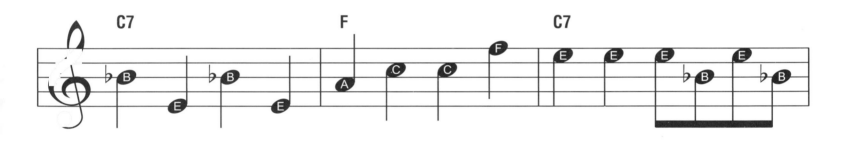

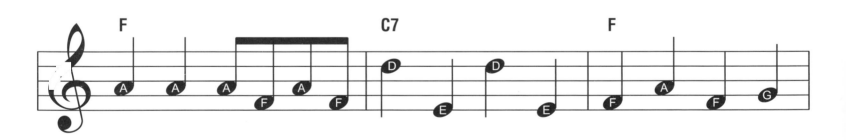

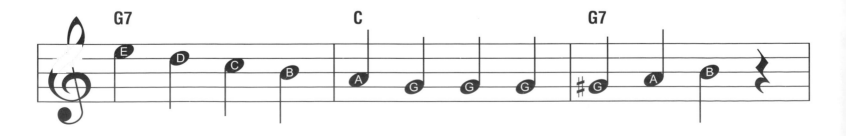

Pomp and Circumstance

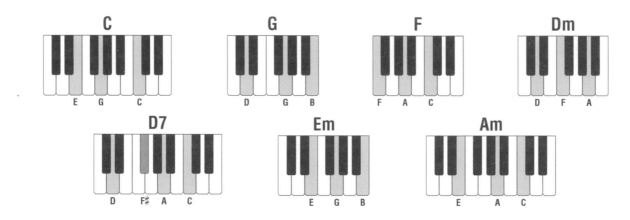

By Edward Elgar

Stately

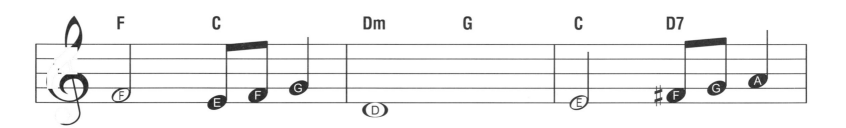

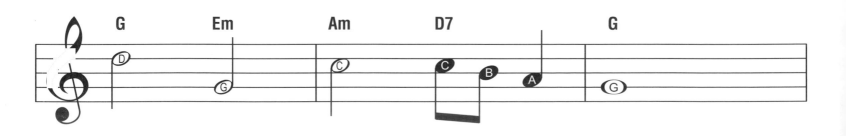

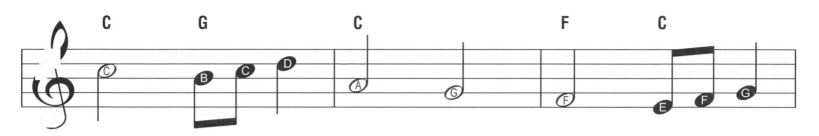
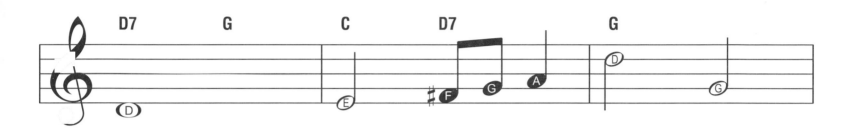
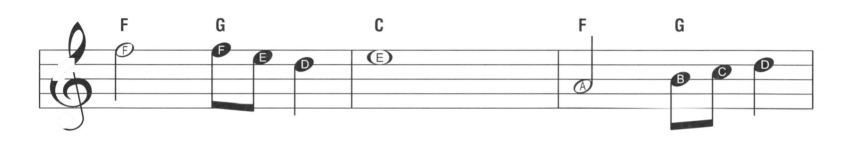
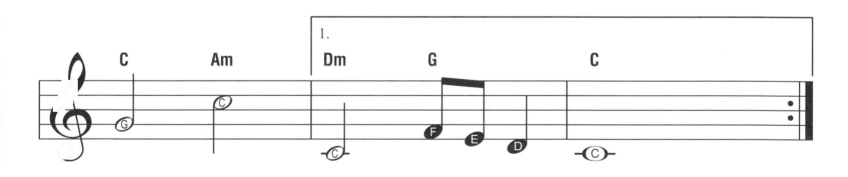
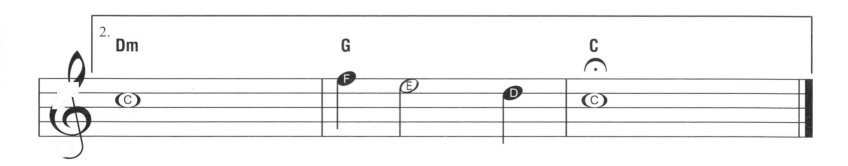

Rondeau

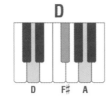

By Jean-Joseph Mouret

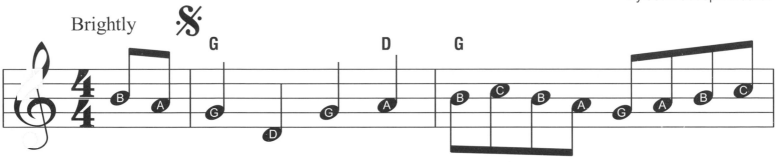

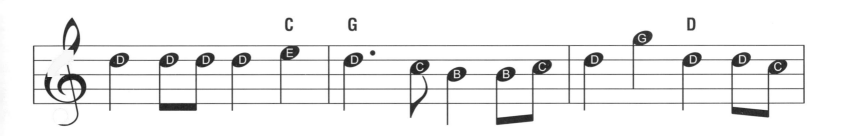

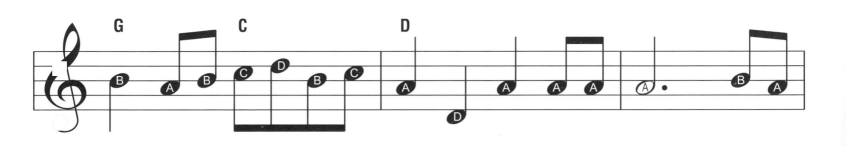

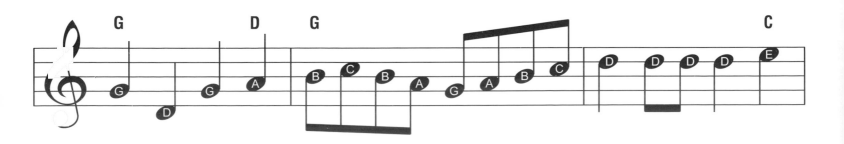

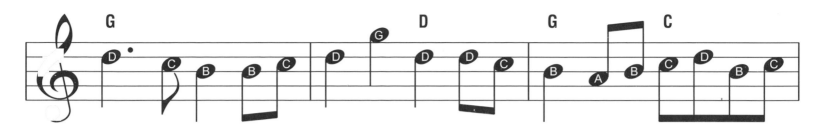

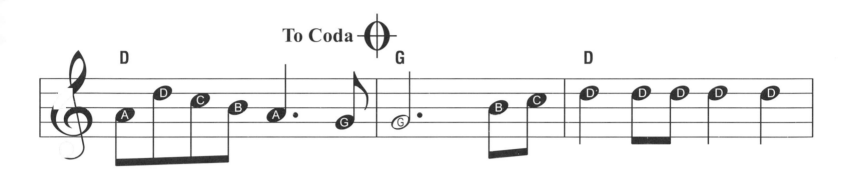

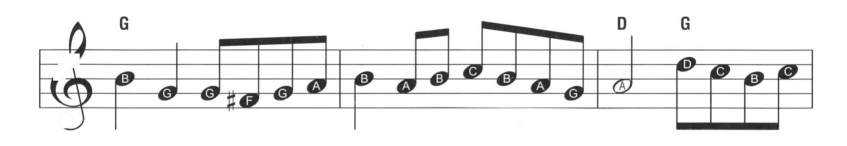

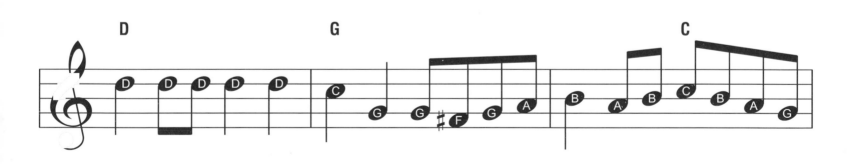

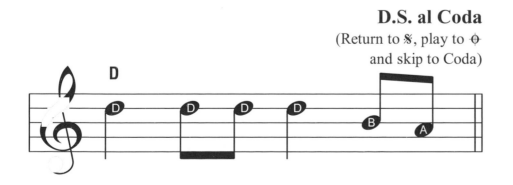

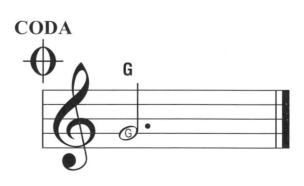

Rondo

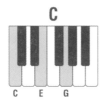
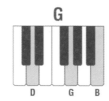
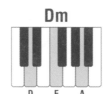
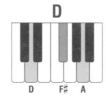

By François Couperin

Moderately fast

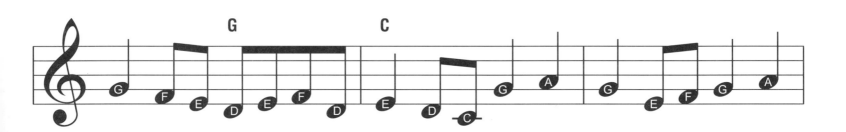

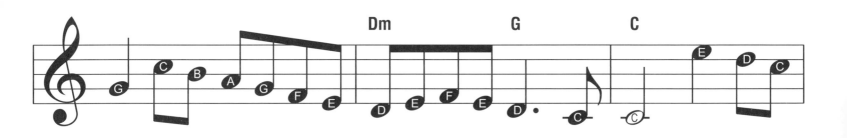

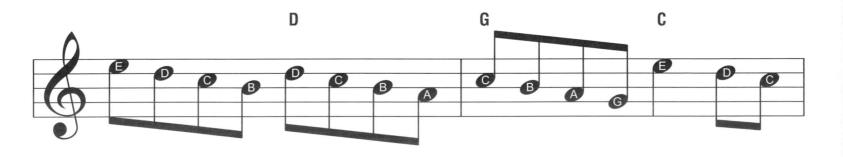

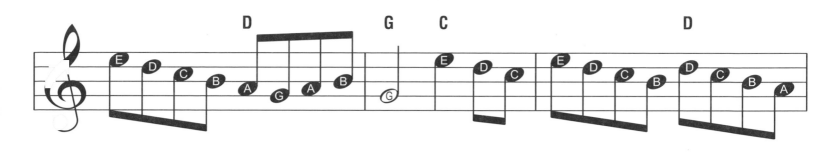

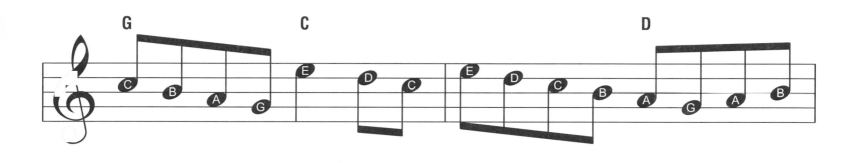

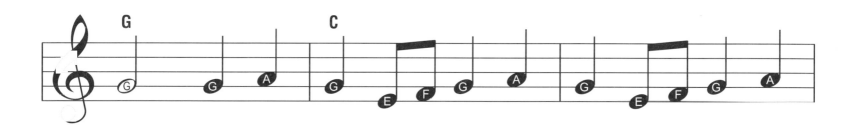

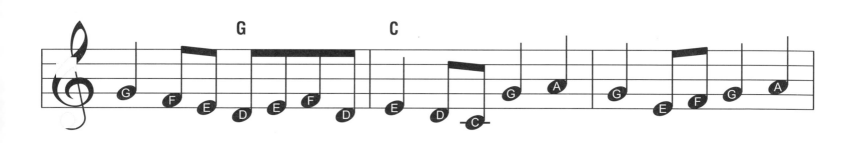

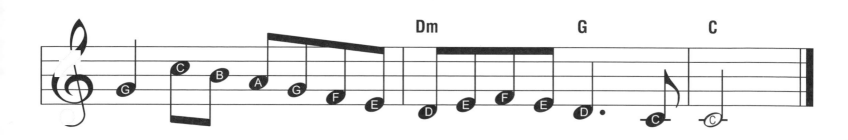

St. Anthony Chorale

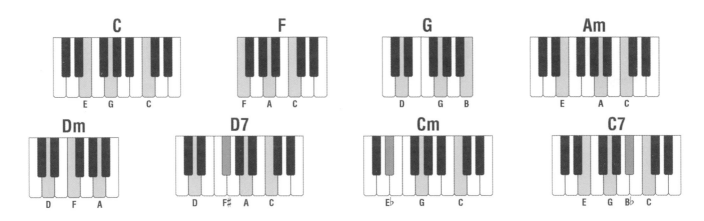

By Franz Joseph Haydn

Stately

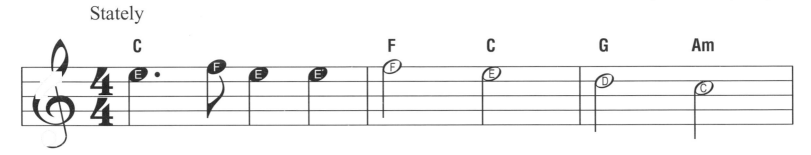

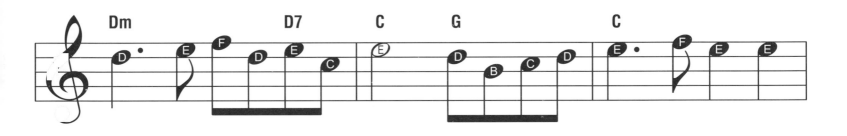

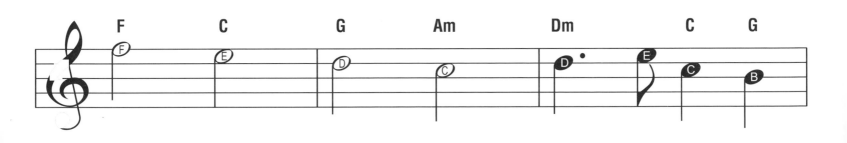

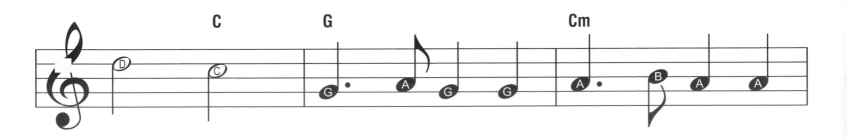

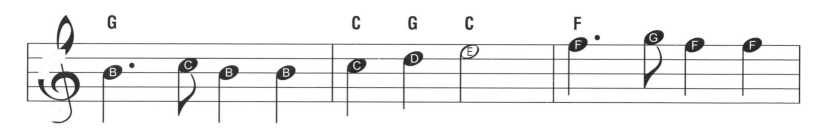

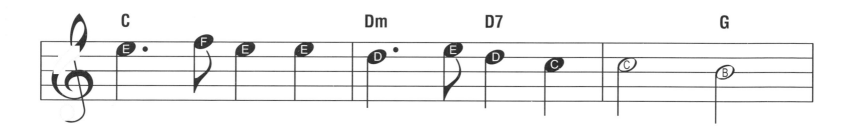

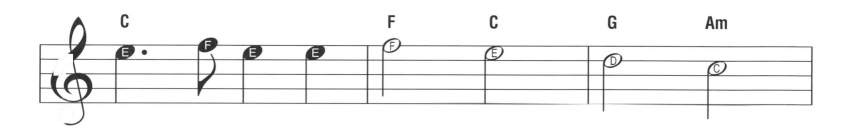

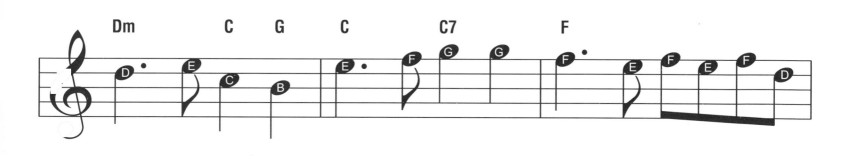

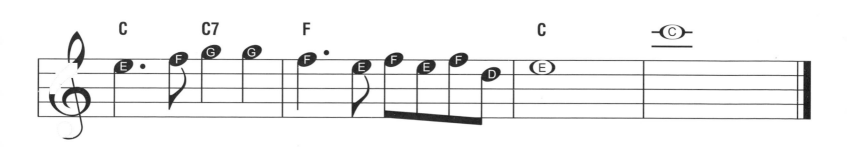

Santa Lucia

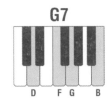
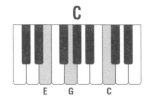
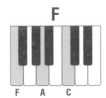

By Teodoro Cottrau

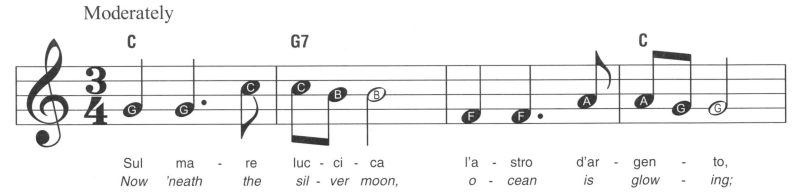

Sul ma - re luc-ci - ca l'a - stro d'ar - gen - to,
Now 'neath the sil - ver moon, o - cean is glow - ing;

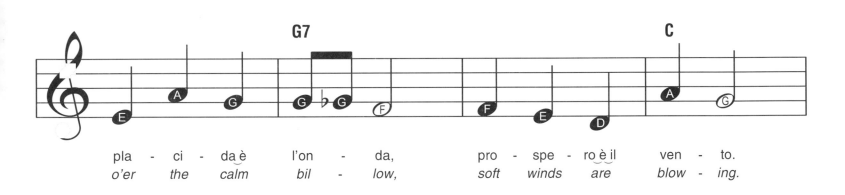

pla - ci - da è l'on - da, pro - spe - ro è il ven - to.
o'er the calm bil - low, soft winds are blow - ing.

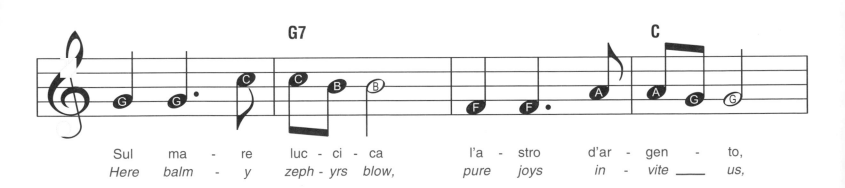

Sul ma - re luc-ci - ca l'a - stro d'ar - gen - to,
Here balm - y zeph - yrs blow, pure joys in - vite ___ us,

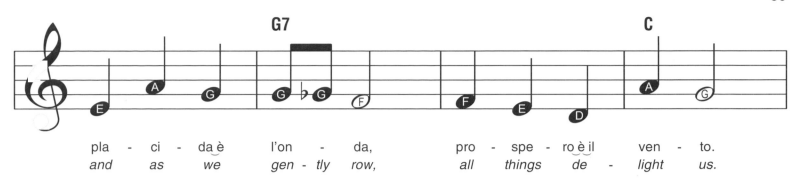

pla - ci - da è l'on - da, pro - spe - ro è il ven - to.
and   as   we   gen - tly   row,   all   things   de - light   us.

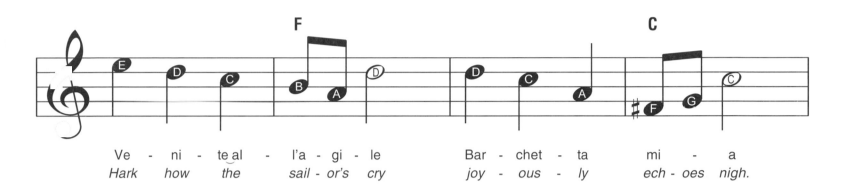

Ve - ni - te al - l'a - gi - le   Bar - chet - ta   mi - a
Hark   how   the   sail - or's   cry   joy - ous - ly   ech - oes   nigh.

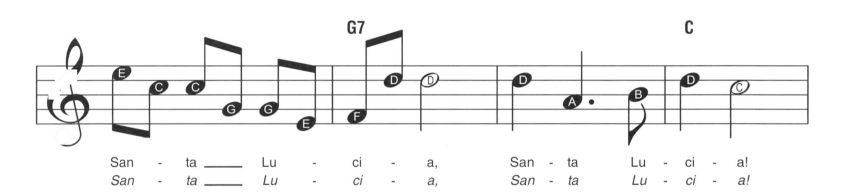

San - ta ____ Lu - ci - a,   San - ta   Lu - ci - a!
San - ta ____ Lu - ci - a,   San - ta   Lu - ci - a!

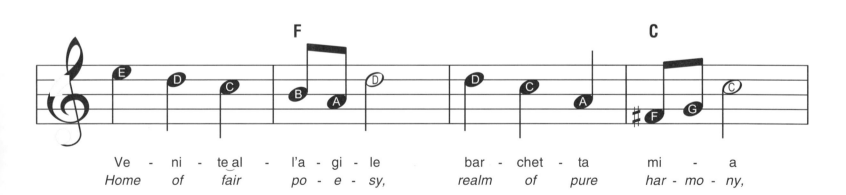

Ve - ni - te al - l'a - gi - le   bar - chet - ta   mi - a
Home   of   fair   po - e - sy,   realm   of   pure   har - mo - ny,

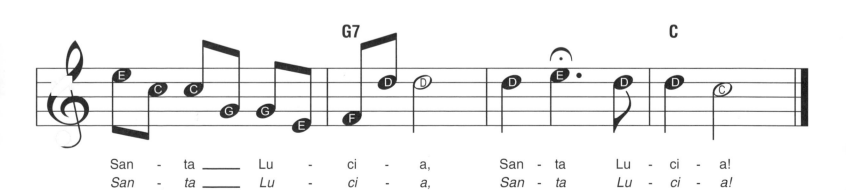

San - ta ____ Lu - ci - a,   San - ta   Lu - ci - a!
San - ta ____ Lu - ci - a,   San - ta   Lu - ci - a!

Serenata

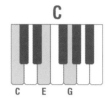
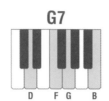
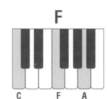

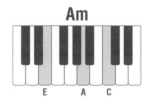

By Enrico Toselli

Moderately, with expression

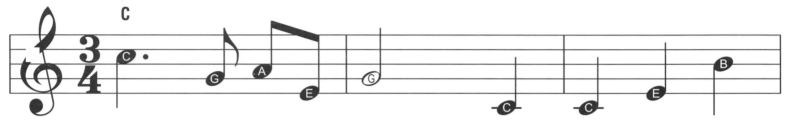

To Coda

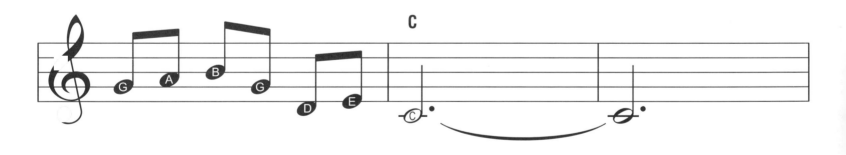

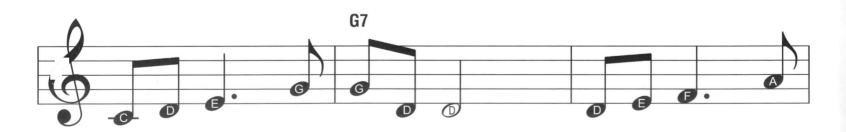

The Skaters Waltz

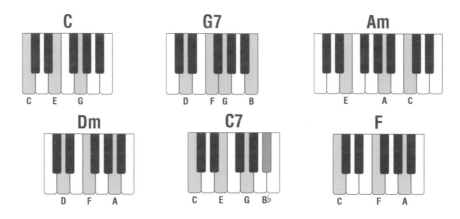

By Emil Waldteufel

Moderate Waltz

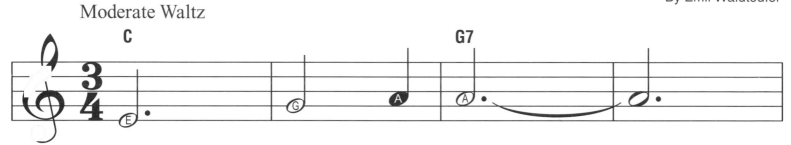

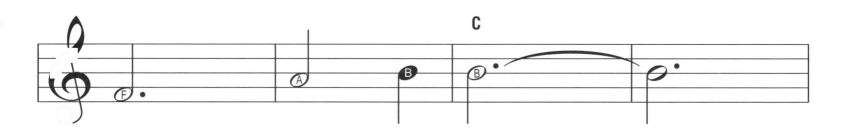

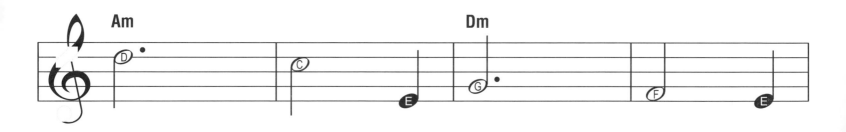

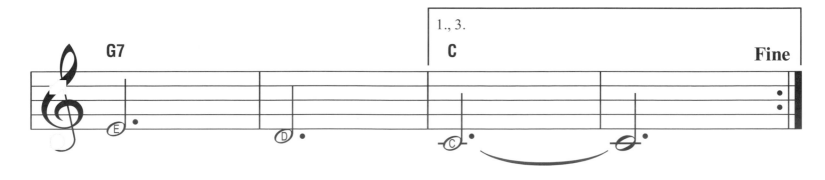

The Sleeping Beauty Waltz

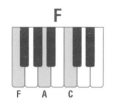
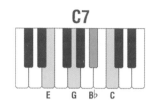
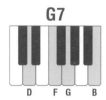
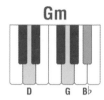
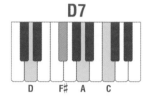

By Pyotr Il'yich Tchaikovsky

Moderately

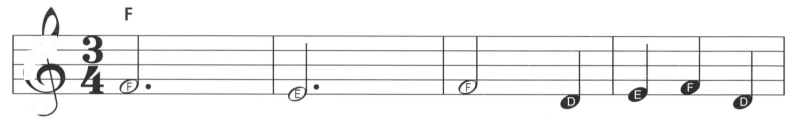

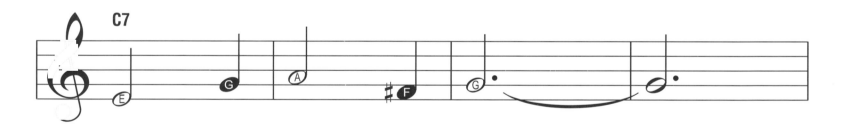

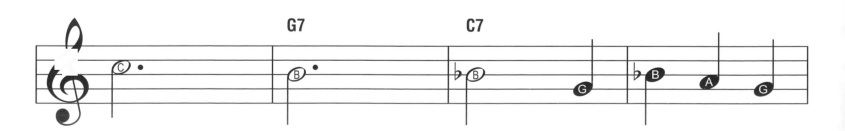

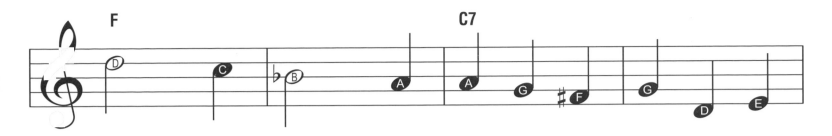

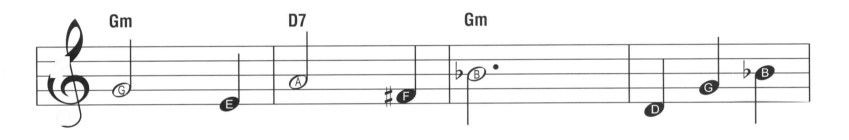

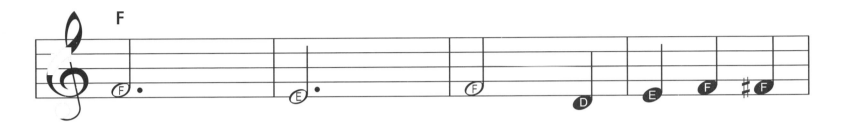

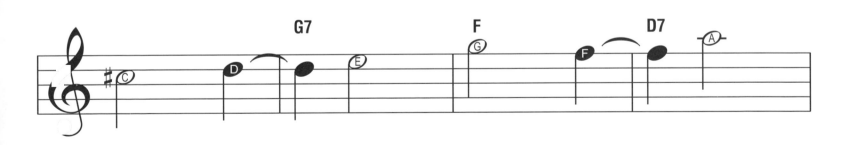

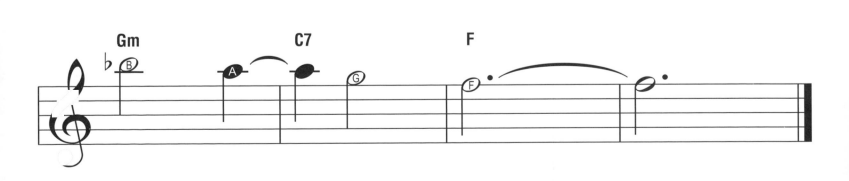

Sonata K. 331
First Movement Theme

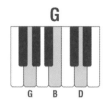
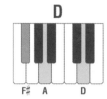
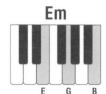
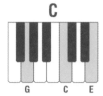

By Wolfgang Amadeus Mozart

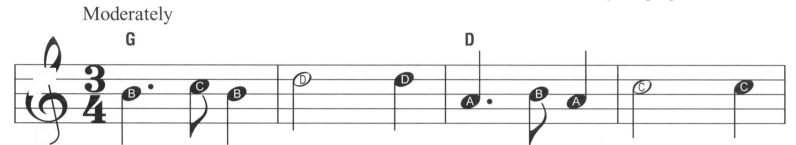

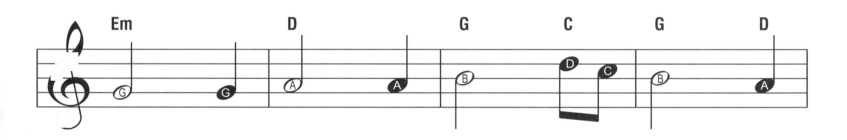

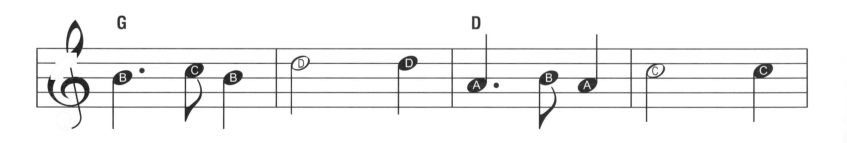

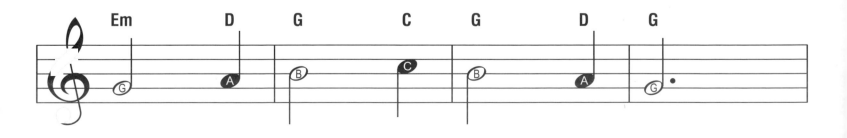

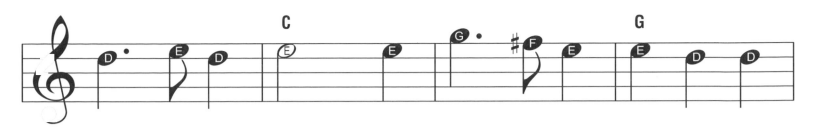

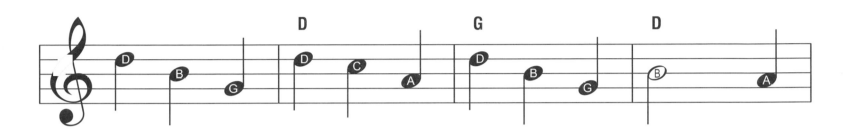

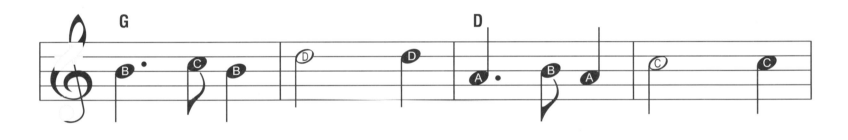

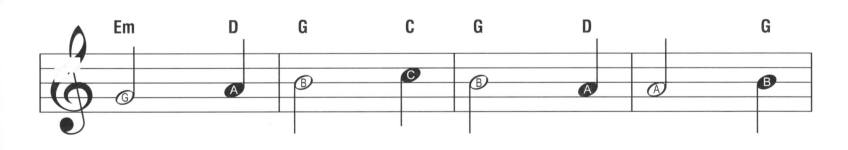

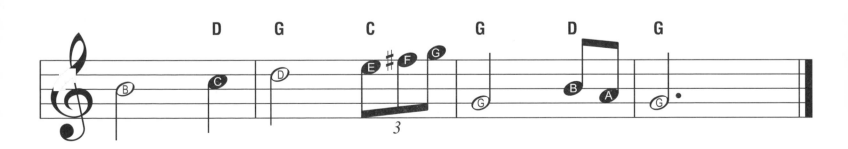

Spring, First Movement Theme

from The Four Seasons

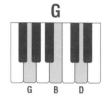
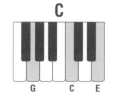

By Antonio Vivaldi

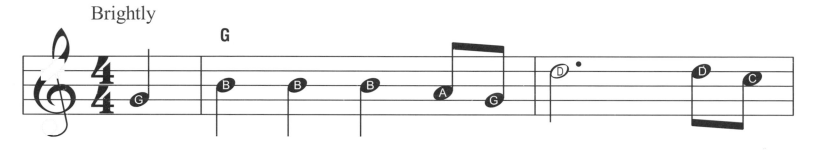

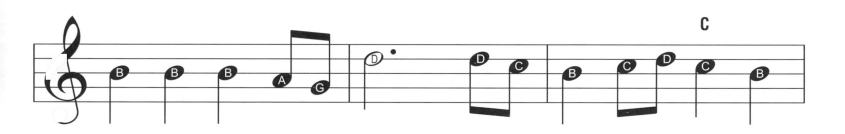

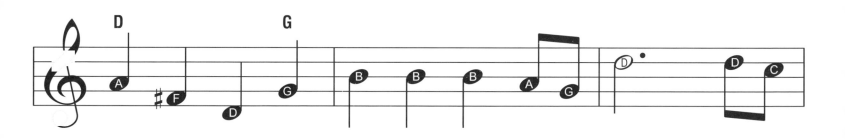

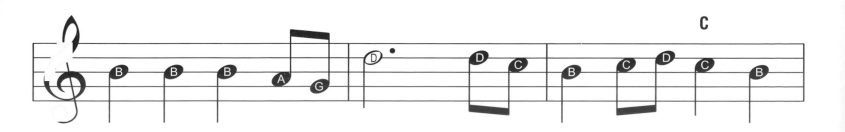

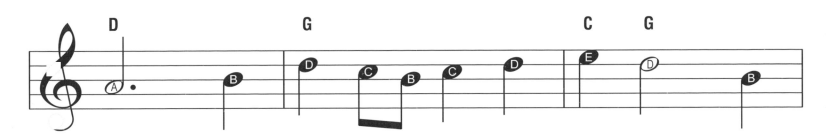

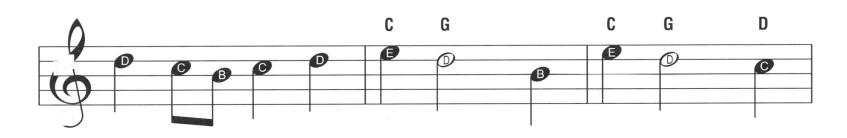

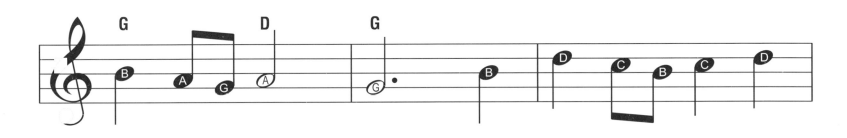

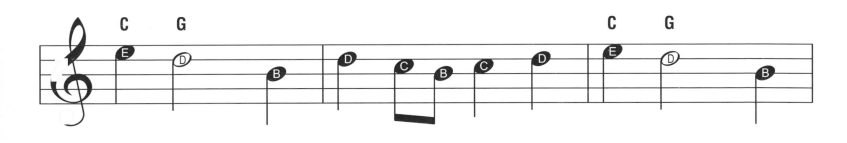

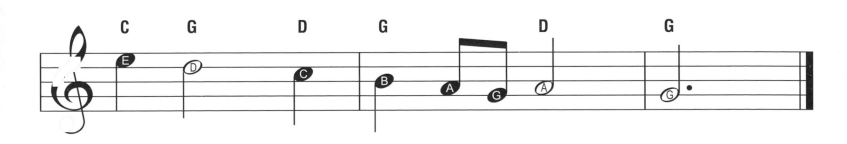

Symphony No. 1
Fourth Movement Theme

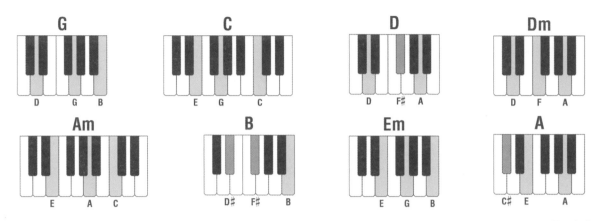

By Johannes Brahms

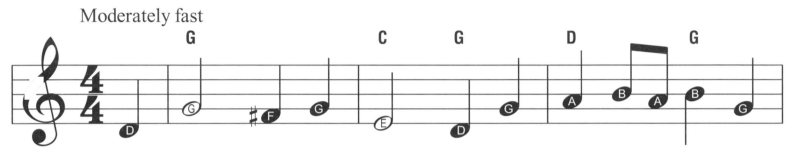

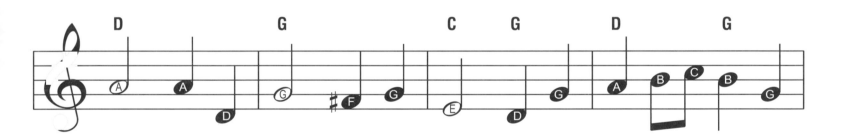

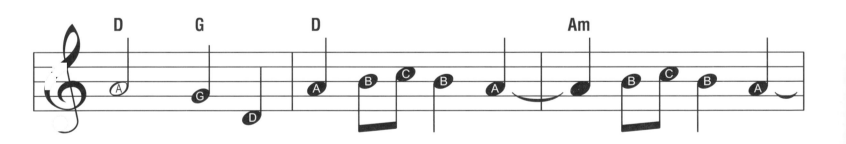

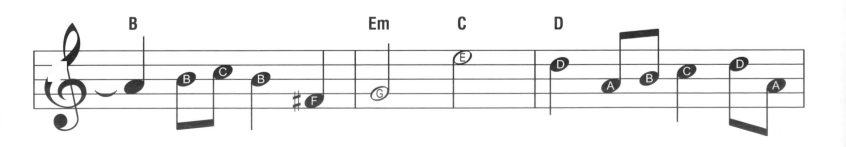

101

Symphony No. 9

("From the New World")
Second Movement Theme

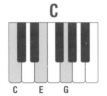
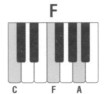
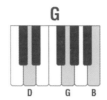
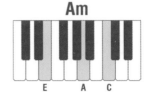

By Antonín Dvořák

Moderately slow

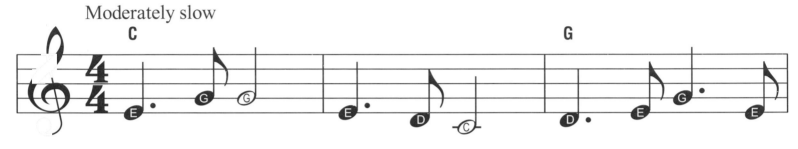

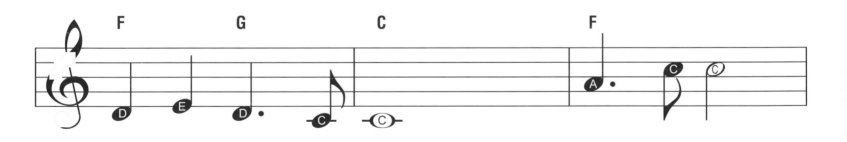

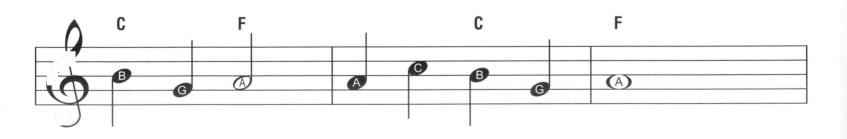

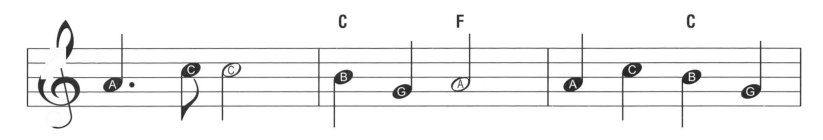

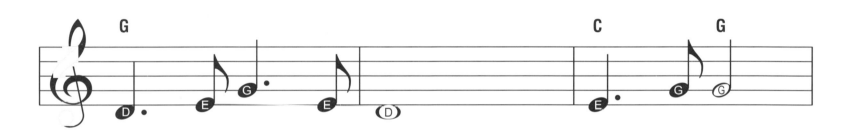

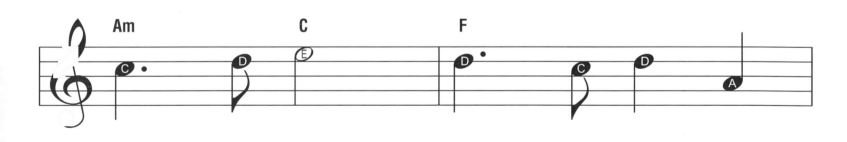

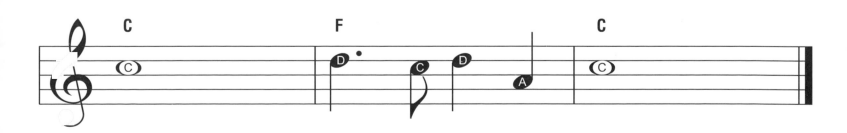

Symphony No. 9
Fourth Movement Theme ("Ode to Joy")

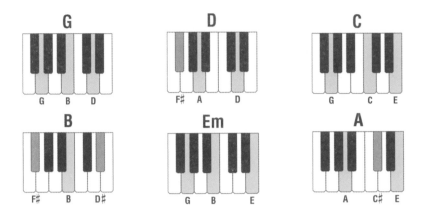

By Ludwig van Beethoven

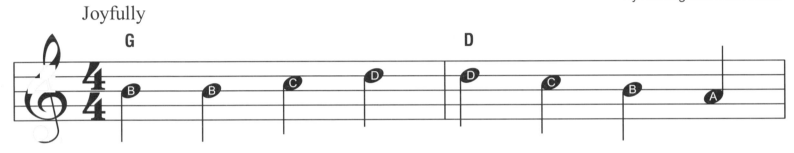

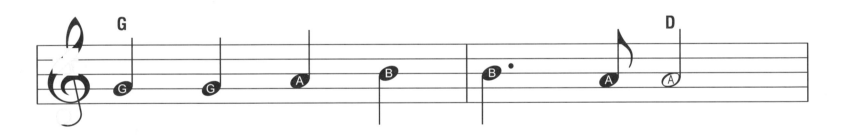

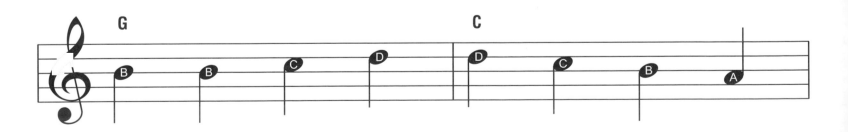

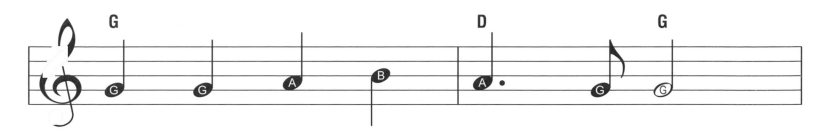

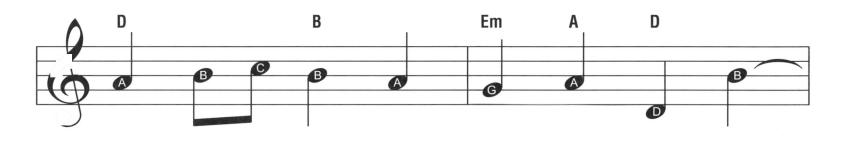

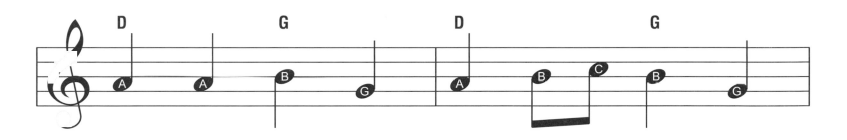

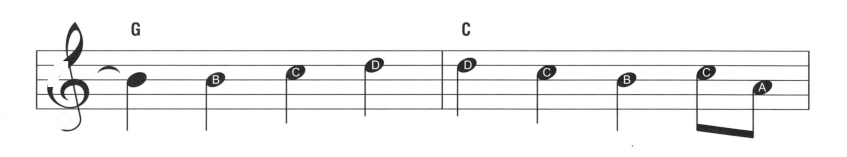

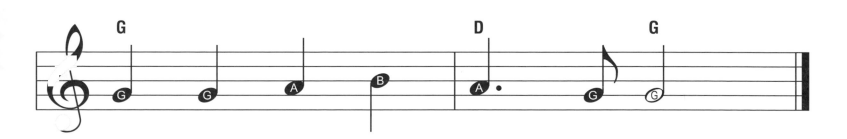

To a Wild Rose

from Woodland Sketches

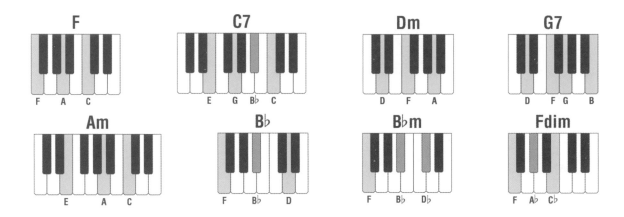

By Edward MacDowell

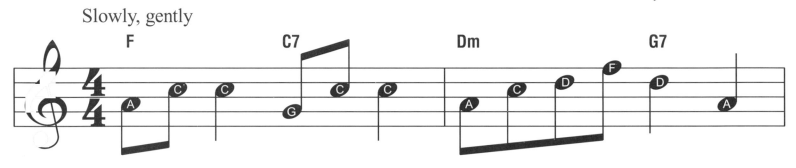

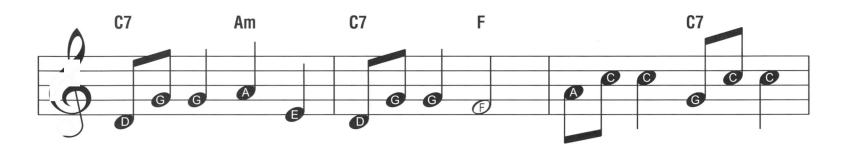

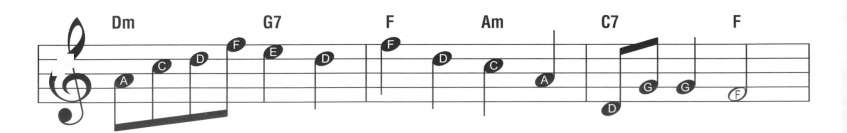

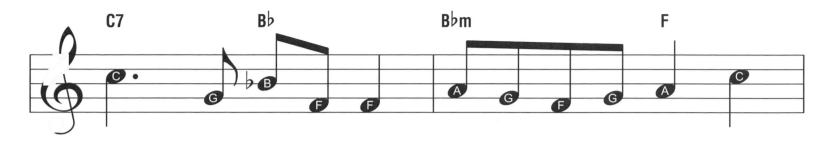

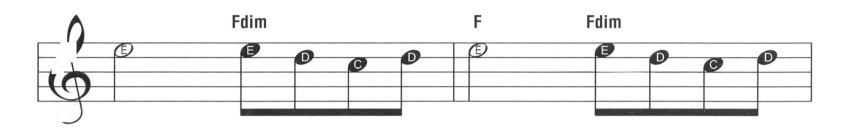

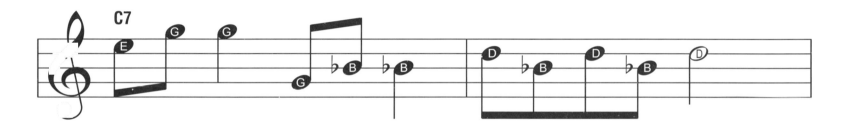

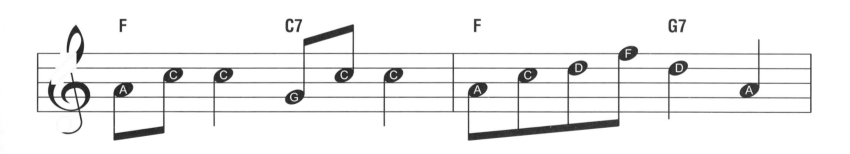

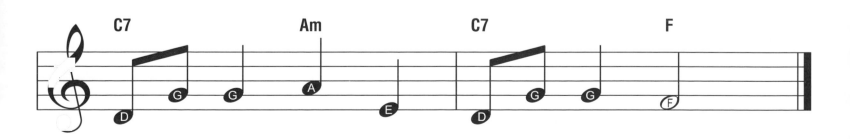

Toyland
from Babes in Toyland

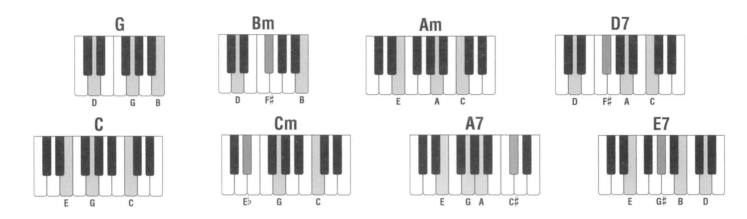

By Victor Herbert

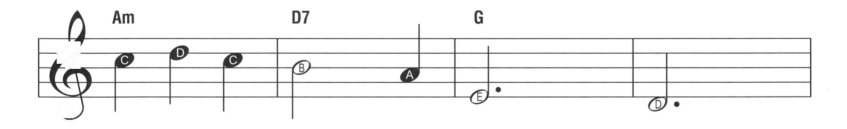

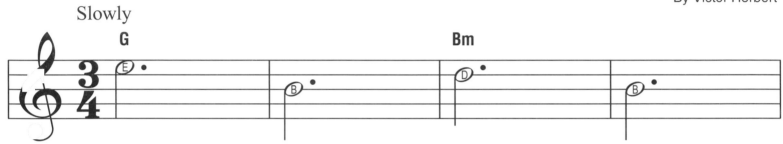

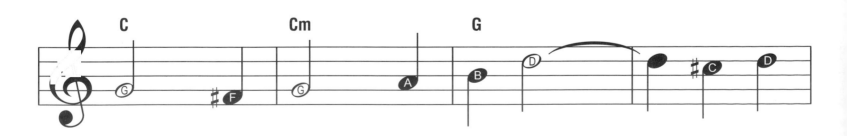

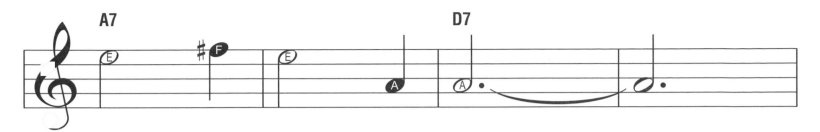

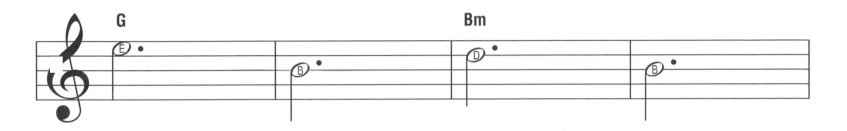

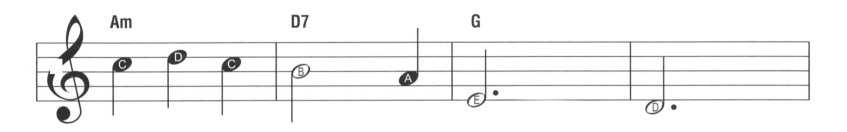

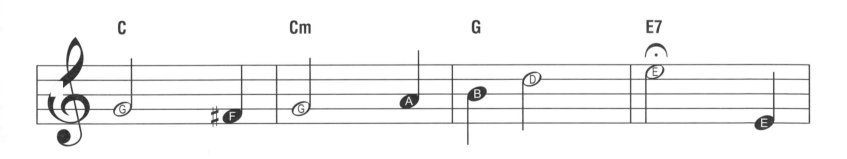

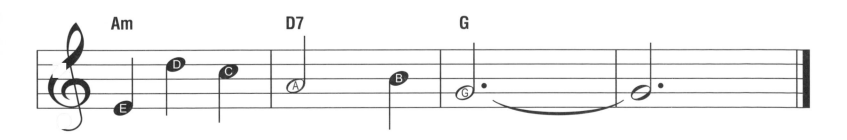

Triumphal March
from Aïda

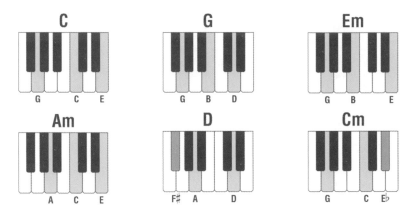

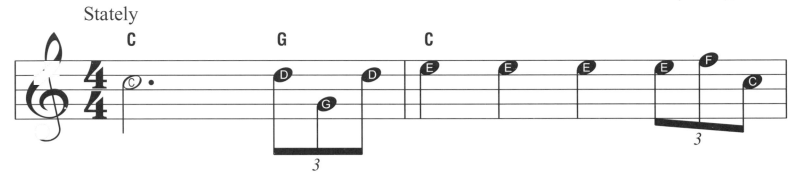

By Giuseppe Verdi

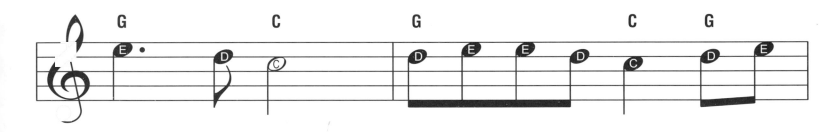

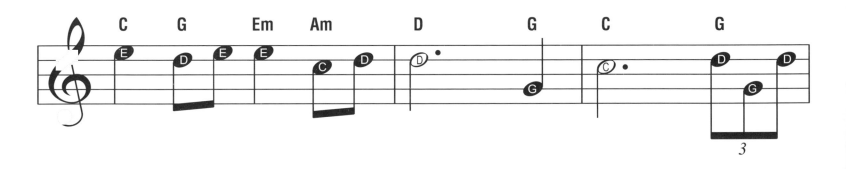

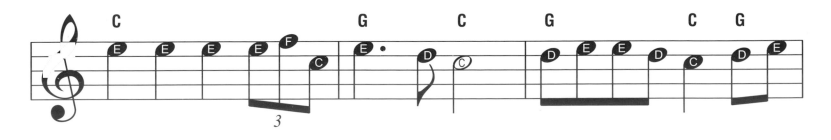

Trumpet Tune

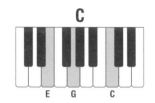 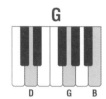 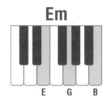 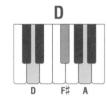 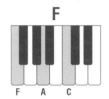

By Henry Purcell

Stately

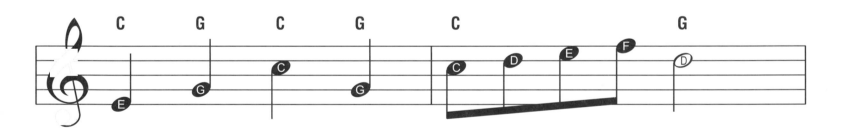

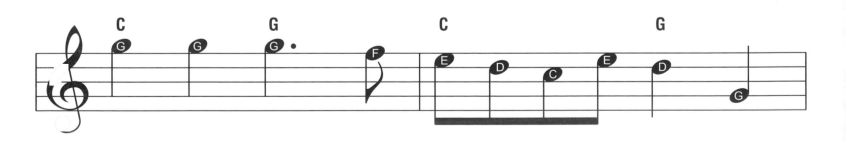

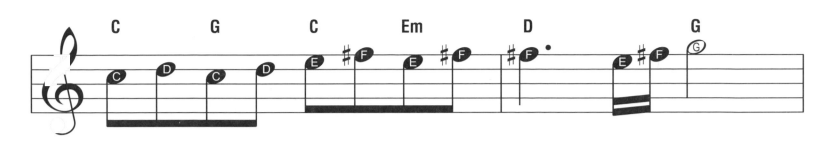

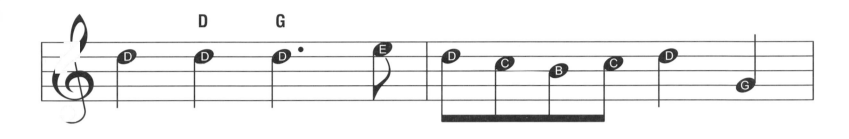

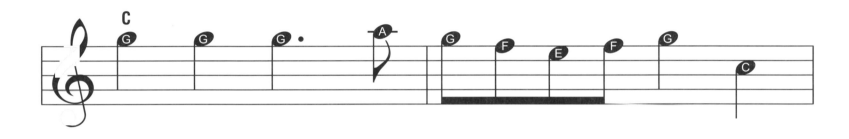

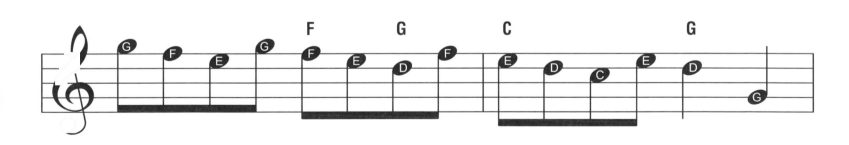

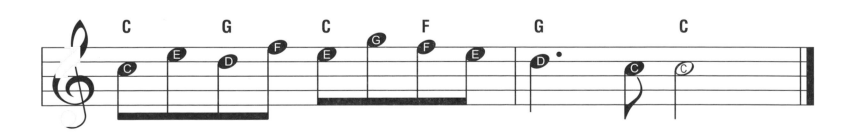

Trumpet Voluntary

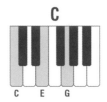
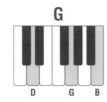
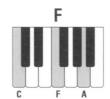
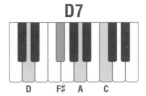

By Jeremiah Clarke

Majestically

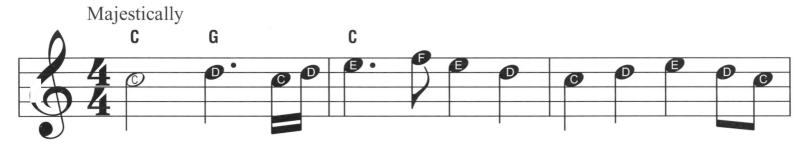

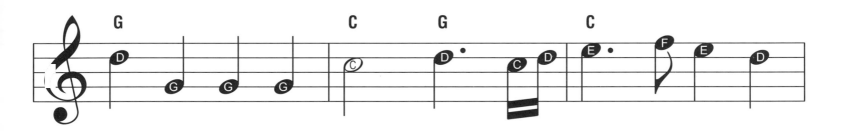

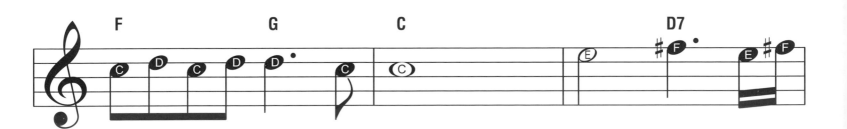

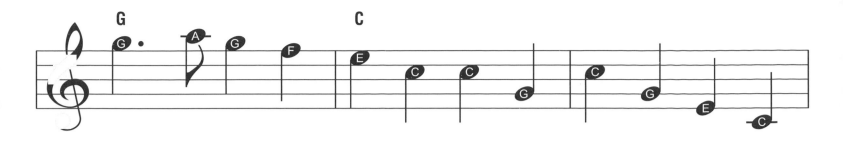

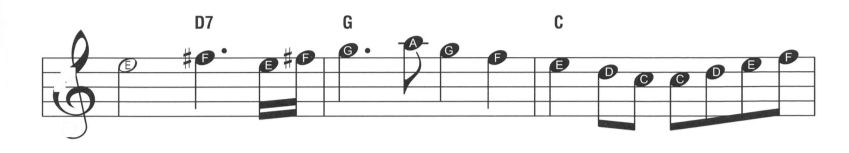

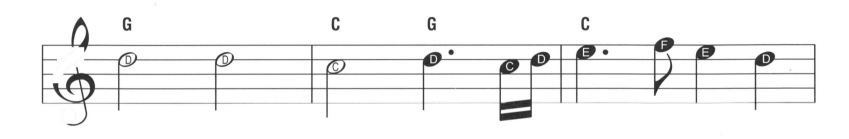

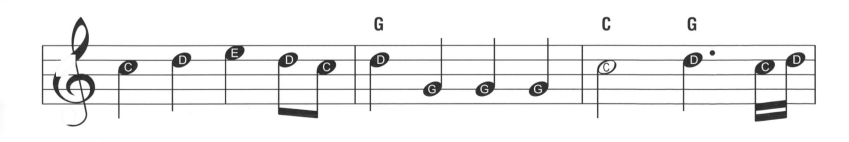

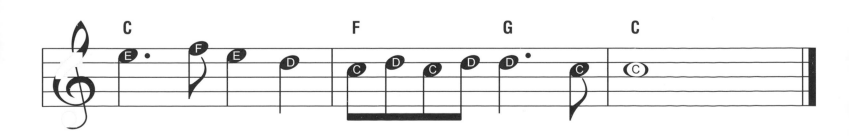

William Tell Overture

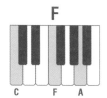
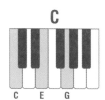
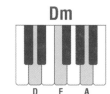
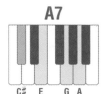

By Gioachino Rossini

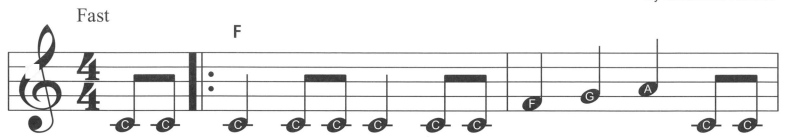

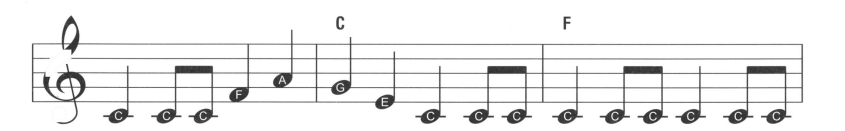

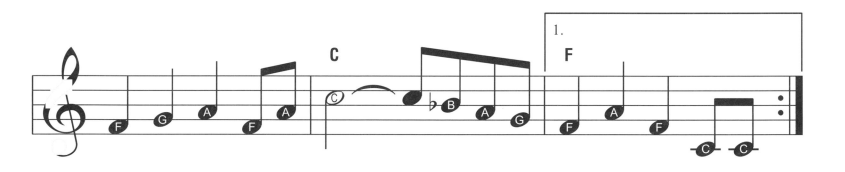

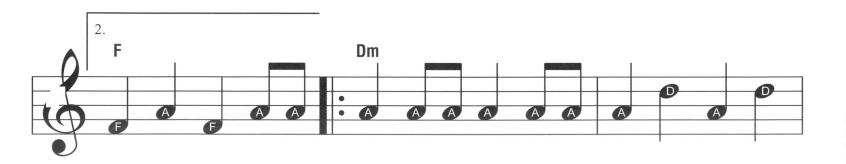

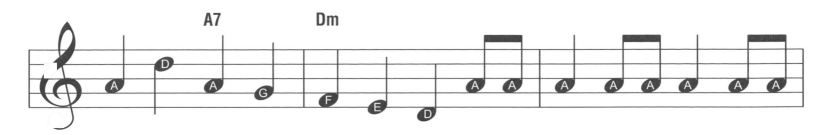

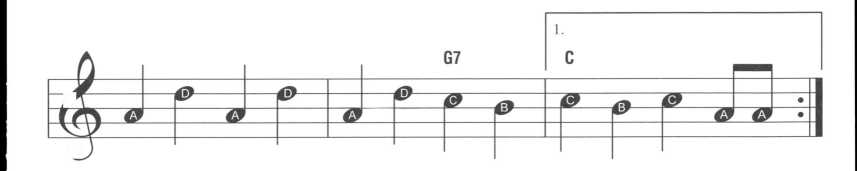

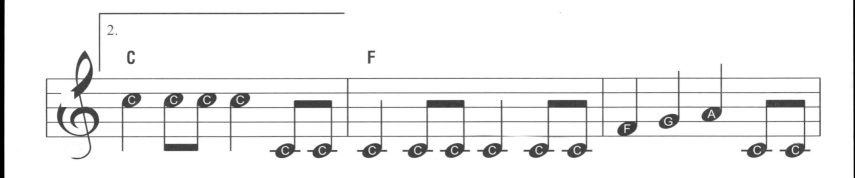

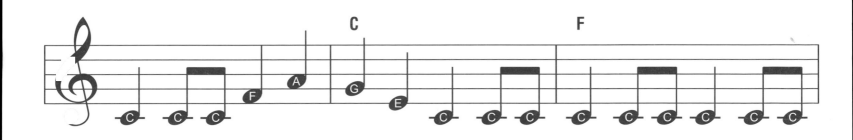

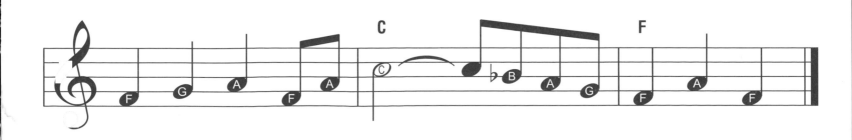

Spring Song
from Songs Without Words

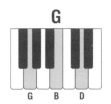

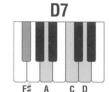
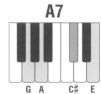
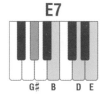

By Felix Mendelssohn

Moderately

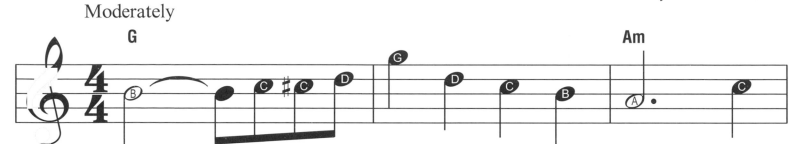

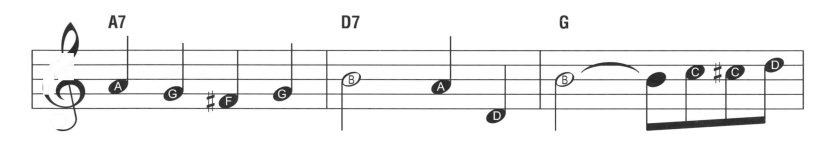

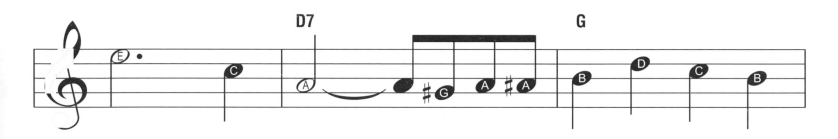

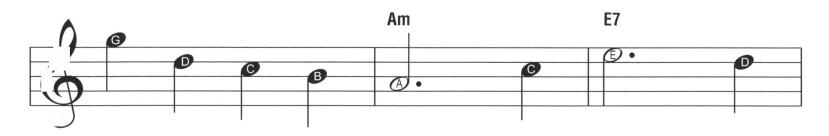

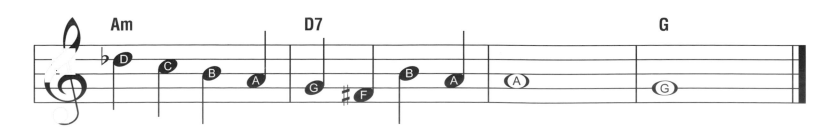